O U T
F R O M
UNDER

OUT
FROM
UNDER

TEXTS BY WOMEN PERFORMANCE ARTISTS

EDITED BY

LENORA CHAMPAGNE

THEATRE COMMUNICATIONS GROUP

Cover art by Janie Geiser, copyright © 1990.

Book design and composition by The Sarabande Press

Library of Congress Cataloging-in-Publication Data
Out from under: texts by women performance artists/edited with an
introduction by Lenora Champagne.
Contents: World without end/Holly Hughes—The father/
Beatrice Roth—From United States/Laurie Anderson—The
constant state of desire/Karen Finley—My Brazil/Rachel
Rosenthal—Teenytown/Laurie Carlos, Jessica Hagedorn, Robbie
McCauley—The survivor and the translator/Leeny Sack—Getting
over Tom/Lenora Champagne—Strange to relate/Fiona Templeton.
ISBN 1-55936-009-7
1. American drama—Women authors. 2. Performance art—United
States. 3. American drama—20th century. 4. Women—Drama.
5. Monologues. I. Champagne, Lenora.
PS628.W6098 1990
812'.540809287—dc20   90-11257
                                                           CIP

First Edition: September 1990
Second Printing: January 1992

ACKNOWLEDGMENTS

The artists in this collection were selected because of the urgency and vitality in their writing. The quality, variety and range of work by women right now made the selection particularly difficult, but we were guided by the desire to include those texts which were most inspiring to us, and which worked best on the page. It is my hope that the publication of this work can help vitalize theatrical discourse, as well as expose these writers to a wider field.

I want to thank TCG for once again supporting innovation in the American theatre by taking the risk of publishing this collection, of inscribing these words in the wider sphere they deserve. For their roles in helping make this book possible, I would particularly like to thank my editor Betty Osborn, whose vision and taste I respect; Terry Nemeth, whose enthusiasm for this project has been unflagging; Janie Geiser, the visual and performance artist whose cover design so vividly expresses the mood of this collection; Jim O'Quinn, who has provided me with the opportunity to continue writing about theatre and performance while I perform and direct my own work; Penny Boyer, with whom I first "tossed around" ideas for the book; and all the artists who sent material for consideration. I would also like to thank the MacDowell Colony, where I was in residence while working on this project.

—*Lenora Champagne*

CONTENTS

OUT FROM UNDER: WOMEN ON SEX AND DEATH AND OTHER THINGS

BY LENORA CHAMPAGNE

Woman must write herself: must write about women and bring women to writing, from which they have been driven away as violently as from their bodies.
Censor the body and you censor breath and speech at the same time.
Woman must put herself into the text—as into the world and into history—by her own movement.

Hélène Cixous
The Laugh of the Medusa

I give people time so they feel their lives moving over their skins. I want a larger arena.

Jenny Holzer
Laments

I've got a beautiful red dress
And you'd look really good standing beside it.
GIRLS?
. . .
We're gonna make it and if we don't—
we're gonna take it.

Laurie Anderson
Beautiful Red Dress

The women represented in this book are performance artists and theatrical soloists who write their own material. The texts collected here are provocative, ambitious and full of (the) body. Beneath the powerful writing is the under-the-skin experience of oppression for being "other"—a Jew, a black, a lesbian, and always, a woman. But these are not the stories of victims. These women are fighters in red dresses. Anger, in the guise of rage or irony, fuels the work; compassion and insight temper it. The artists express, with urgency, visions of the possible that are sometimes hopeful, often frightening.

SETTING OUT

When tracing the course of twentieth-century writing and artwork by women, one often finds a trail of blood. From Susan Glaspell to Marsha Norman, Lillian Hellman to Marguerite Duras, Sophie Treadwell to Irene Fornes, Frida Kahlo to Ana Mendieta, Martha Graham to Pina Bausch, in work after work women's silence implodes into violence, often manifested as murder or suicide. Society's definition of normalcy is represented as distorted or perverted. Home is no haven, but a dangerous place, a suffocating enclosure, a cage to fly from.

During the 1970s, in the wake of feminism, some women in the art world had had enough of this silence and its repressive consequences, enough of normative feminine behavior, enough of staying at home. Women began breaking taboos, talking about and doing the unspeakable, fleeing the kitchen and bedroom to express their interior lives and explore the outside world. In her explorations of space, Joan Jonas set mirrors into remote Canadian landscapes; in New York performances, she split her persona among various actors, themselves masked and mirrored on video monitors. Carolee Schneemann combined body art with visual images and writing, using films, slides and nudity in her challenging work. In 1975 she performed *Interior Scroll*, in which she read a text about her experiences of discrimination in the art world (a structuralist filmmaker criticized her films for their "clutter" and "persistence of feelings"), extracting it from her vagina. Other artists put on flamboyant, theatrical personas and went around in them. Eleanor Antin donned a beard and called herself the King of Spain; Linda Montano, a former nun, made daily expeditions as the Chicken Woman. Lynn Hershman created an alternate self, Roberta Breitmore, who had her own social security number and driver's license, and a separate social life and therapist. Creating a series of imagined film stills, Cindy Sherman photographed herself as movie stars.

Trying out personas, especially those of men or socially marginal women, was both a personal exploration and a taking or undermining of power by inhabiting images of it, and can be seen as a kind of social and personal research. In this challenge to authority, artists were representing themselves in images created as alternatives to or comments upon the traditional images and roles they had inherited.

The women's movement, with its consciousness-raising groups, encouraged the exposure of personal material in public. Personal history was turned into art by decisions about structure and form; new structures and forms arose with the expression of this personal material. Sometimes this work, which created an intimate relationship with the audience because of the nature of the material revealed, was criticized as "confessional." But this view overlooks the difference between confession and revelation. The role of the spectator was not that of pardoner, but of witness. In work based on the direct expression of the unspeakable—what is left unsaid in the culture—the author/performer becomes a mediator between (or medium for) this knowledge and the spectator. In any case, these "confessional" women found it ironic that the same form was praised when male colleagues began performing monologues.

LEARNING FROM

The performance-art form has subversive origins and tendencies. Performance art's roots are not in theatre, but in the art world and in dissent. Contemporary performance has precedents in the avant-garde movements of the early twentieth century that challenged established standards and definitions of art and sought to shake up social conventions with shocking, outrageous behavior in public appearances. In the seventies the predominant impulses of performance were conceptual and/

or autobiographical, in response to conceptual art and feminism and in reaction to minimalism. Much of this art was real-time based and process oriented, challenging the commercial-object status of the art-work. Instead of creating a product for sale, artists focused on perception: perceiving time, perceiving difference. Often these performances were not repeatable.

As performance moved from artists' lofts into galleries, museums and other art spaces, the form changed, in terms of both economic structure and style. Theatre artists who wanted to stretch conventional forms became aware of the option of "doing your own show" and began working in art- and dance-world venues. (Probably because of the conceptual orientation of postmodern dance, the dance world was for a long time more receptive to performance art than was theatre.)

Today, performance art is gradually moving into theatres, in addition to clubs and performance spaces which present theatre and dance. The performance rituals, persona explorations and time-based work that characterized the form in the seventies have for the most part been replaced by work ranging from "new vaudeville" to comedy monologues to the punkish, "bad-child" East Village aesthetic (exemplified by DanceNoise, a performance duo). Museum or gallery performances, such as those of the V-Girls, are often ironic challenges to authority and contemporary theory; alternatively, as in the recent work of Constance de Jong and Joan Jonas, they are complex, elegant interplays of live performance and video images. Irony has become the prevalent perform-ance attitude, and is more often seen today than the raw emotional intensity and sincerity of earlier work. In the seventies the focus was on the integrity of the concept or idea and on intimate sharing of a private ritual with the audience. Today's growing audiences for performance often seem to want to be entertained and stimulated rather than chal-lenged by the concepts or emotions behind the work.

UNDER GROWTH

Yet much contemporary performance, with its use of explicit revelations and imagery, still retains the power to provoke and shock audiences out of their complacency. At P.S. 122 or The Kitchen or Franklin Furnace, one might see Karen Finley pouring a can of kidney beans over her forearm as she talks about menstrual blood, or Nancy Reilly playing out the lowlife scenario of a coked-out barmaid who degrades herself for "an inch of pennies," or Robbie McCauley standing naked on an auction block as she rages about racial injustice. In the move from art galleries to nightclubs, performance became grittier, and the current emphasis on showmanship and compelling performance style tends to favor artists with theatrical flair.

Some of the strongest performance artists in the 1980s have been the theatrical soloists. Many of these performer/writers have powerful, direct and original voices that cut to the heart of things; some of them are funny and most are angry. Karen Finley and Holly Hughes take on sex and death more radically than their male contemporaries; Fiona Templeton works a kind of alchemy, fragmenting the matter of language and identity; Leeny Sack, Laurie Carlos and Jessica Hagedorn explore and explode racial outrage and the marks that history leaves on the self. These are just a few of the female artists who provide and provoke the intellectual stimulation, gritty gutsiness and fundamental passions that make it possible to experience catharsis in the postmodern era, and that inspire one to take action.

Like Carolee Schneemann's *Interior Scroll*, the writing by these women comes from a deep, dark place. We're looking into ourselves, looking at the world around us, and letting our monsters out. Listen for the rage; you'll hear it. Listen again, and you'll hear laughter—the light side of the dark, the surplus of pleasure from that powerful release.

POSTSCRIPT

As this book is about to be printed, the arts community is reeling from and outraged by the announcement last week that four of the eighteen artists recommended for funding by the National Endowment for the Arts panel for the solo performance category have been denied fellowships by NEA Chairman John Frohnmayer and the National Council on the Arts, clearly for political reasons. Five of the artists included in this collection—Karen Finley, Holly Hughes, Rachel Rosenthal, Beatrice Roth and myself—were among those recommended for funding by the panel; two of them—Finley and Hughes—were later denied support by the Chairman after a phone poll of the Council.

Normally, one would like to feel pleased about recognition, but the decision to exclude and blacklist four artists in order to appease radicals on the far right is an ominous turn of events that, viewed in conjunction with recent inroads on a woman's right to choose and increased incidents of homophobic and racist violence in the nation, requires immediate action and ongoing vigilance. We're in a dangerous and difficult period, in which difference is threatened, and freedom of expression challenged.

Rachel Rosenthal, in refusing to accept her fellowship, spoke of the specter of Nazism conjured up for her by the efforts to censor artists contained in the language in the NEA contract and by the decision to reject four artists whose work is sometimes sexually explicit and confrontational: "The first thing the Nazis tried to do is silence the artists and intellectuals." For many of us, the specter being raised is that of the blacklists of the fifties, the hysteria of the McCarthy era.

As repression lifts in the Eastern Bloc, are we going to let it settle on us? The ongoing attacks on individual artists, whose work has been repeatedly taken out of context, are a sinister suggestion of further repression to come. A few political and religious extremists are looking for scapegoats and sacrificial lambs close to home. But we aren't going to be sheep.

—L.C.
July 4, 1990

OUT FROM UNDER

WORLD WITHOUT END

HOLLY HUGHES

HOLLY HUGHES

Holly Hughes was born in 1955 in Saginaw, Michigan, "the navy bean capital of the world." She is the older of two sisters. "My mother (who died in 1987) was a depressed housewife, which was plenty of work. We raised her. I never knew my father, even though he lived in the same house. He worked at General Motors, where they made noise." One of her ancestors was killed at the Battle of the Little Big Horn. "I come from a long line of bloodthirsty military colonizers, which prepared me well for performance art and gave me the correct stance to do battle on St. Marks Place."

A Jesus freak in high school, Hughes got a B.A. in painting at Kalamazoo College. She moved to New York in 1979 to continue painting at the Feminist Art Institute.

> It really seemed like this time when you could make these big steel vaginas and erect them in the city, if I may use the verb, and somehow just topple the whole patriarchal system. Those were the days when people said "patriarchy" the way they say "shit" now.

Ideological problems and conflicts soon broke up the group she was in at the institute. "We were so blindered by our desire for perfect sisterhood that we just couldn't get along as human beings." She supported herself by waitressing, lived in Queens and stopped painting.

> I was still sniffing around for a women's community. I saw this sign up about the WOW Festival. This was 1981 and I had moved to the East Village and there was this festival of women performance artists happening . . . . Some of it wasn't very good but the sense of humor and sense of experimentation felt so vital. It didn't feel gallery-ified, like so many of the other performances I'd seen that looked like they were happening under glass.

Hughes began volunteering at the WOW Cafe, a lesbian/feminist performance club in the East Village, and was soon writing plays—*The Well of Horniness, The Lady Dick*—in which she also performed. Later, she moved to such venues as Performance Space 122 with *Dress Suits for Hire* (performed by Lois Weaver and Peggy Shaw of Split Britches) and her solo, *World without End*.

Hughes is an articulate, powerful woman, small in stature and fired with intelligent presence. Her hennaed blunt cut brings to mind Louise Brooks, and in performance Hughes has the seductive quality of the legendary Lulu. The flat tones of her native Midwest are animated by the pleasure and confidence with which she caresses words. Clearly a woman who claims language and sexuality on her own terms, she seems to be in command of both.

> Just because men have exploited and colonized the female body onstage doesn't mean that we cannot put on our own versions. A lot of feminist theatre critics and academics feel that female sexuality can never be represented onstage without it becoming a peep show. I really disagree. You have to take the risk.

Hughes characteristically employs metaphor and lyrical imagery, combined with a sharp irony that undercuts any sentimentality. Although she has clearly experienced her share of childhood pain and adult disappointment, she uses her imagination to transform these experiences and to create myths she can use.

There have been a couple of staged versions of *World without End*. The first included a number of ladies-in-waiting—women in lingerie who hauled a giant pink pig, from which the girdle-and-corset-clad Hughes popped out. During most of the performance, she sat in a slipper chair as she addressed the audience. In the later version, she wore a red raw-silk dress and soon shifted from an internal, self-questioning tone to a direct, almost confrontational relationship with the audience. Overall, the staging was simple and relied on Hughes' presence and focus rather than on spectacular effects.

World without End, *commissioned by Performance Space 122 through a grant by the New York State Council on the Arts, premiered at P.S. 122 in May 1989. Holly Hughes has performed it in San Diego, Los Angeles, San Francisco, Washington, D.C., Boston, Seattle and other cities. The piece was directed by Kate Stafford, Karen Crumley was dramaturg, lighting was by Lori E. Seid, and costume and set design was by Christine Vlasak. The original music was created (with Beverly Bronson and Vincent Girot) and performed by Sharon Jane Smith. Special thanks to Donna Evans and the Downtown Art Company. Hughes' published texts include the plays* Dress Suits for Hire (The Drama Review, *Spring 1989) and* The Well of Horniness, *included in the collection* Out Front *(Grove Press, 1988).*

WORLD WITHOUT END

in memory of my mother
June W. Hughes

An overstuffed wingback chair upstage right, facing the audience. A small end table is placed to the left of the chair. On the table is a china vase with flowers. The flowers could be anything seasonal and old-fashioned, say peonies or big juicy mums. Roses would be fabulous of course, if you can afford them. Just to the left and slightly downstage of the end table is a huge pot of hydrangeas.

Blackout. In the darkness a woman enters the set. The audience can hear her heels clicking on the floor. She is carrying a composition book, which she tosses onto the chair.

Lights up, a special on the chair area. Make it flattering. The woman is seated on the floor behind the chair, with her back to the audience. A leg sticks out on either side of the chair. During the following section the woman speaks with a steely sort of calmness. She is laying her cards on the table, she has just recently crossed some personal Rubicon. She gestures with her hands as she speaks.

Okay. Here's the deal.
I'm going to tell you a story. It's just a little story, nothing heavy.
A story about a bird.
But the thing is that right now I can't remember the name of that bird.
Jesus! What is the name of that bird?
All I remember is: she had a nest under the eaves, she was very ordinary
    looking, you know—small, brown.
I don't remember seeing the male around.
But she came back. Every year. The same bird.

Okay! Maybe it wasn't the same one as when I was a kid, but it probably
   was her daughter.
Maybe even her daughter's daughter.
Okay! So the thing is: some nights my father'd come home drunk.
   There'd be the sounds of insults, breaking glass, you know.
The usual family stuff, right?
And I'd open the window very carefully because she might have a family.
And I'd look at that nest.
Sure looked like a piece of shit to me!
But she came back every year.
I thought that could mean this was a safe place after all.
Or it could mean she didn't know any better. She didn't know what else to
   do but go on living in the mess her mother'd made.
We don't know.
We don't even know her name.
I bet my mother does. I'm going to ask her. When I get the chance.
She's always calling me, Jesus! Can you believe it!
I'm completely grown up and she's dead! What's there to say about it?
Get over it, Mom!
If she calls tonight, you answer the phone. You ask her for me:
What is the name of that bird?
She'll know the one I mean.
We only had one bird in our family.

> *Blackout. Lights up. The woman is sitting in the chair. Sitting, what
> am I saying, she's lounging. One leg is draped over the side, she's sunk
> down into the cushions. She's wearing a red silk off-the-shoulder
> number, possibly her mother's, and gold high heels. She's just stepped
> out of a Balthus painting. The composition book is open on her lap
> and she reads from it.*

What could I have been thinking about?
Nothing. I wasn't thinking, I was cooking.
I didn't even have a phone. Whenever Mom'd start calling around for me,
   I'd just get out the big knife. Start chopping up everything I could get
   my hands on, everything that wasn't nailed down.
He'd watch, laugh, roll a joint.
You see he was a prep cook. I was just short order.
He really knew his way around a kitchen.

He had a respect for vegetables I didn't understand at the time.

I don't think he knew I had a mother.

I never told him.
I certainly didn't tell him I had a girlfriend.
Well, I used to.

Look, I don't think there's anything wrong with me paying for her
    abortion. I was the one who loved her, not him!

But after the third one, all I wanted to do was cook.
She was a vegetarian so I made sure I was always up to my elbows in
    chopped meat.
I'd go into the walk-in and he'd say: "Need a hand?"
And I'd say: "No. This is something I've got to do for myself."
I'd see those big cardboard cartons of frozen beef patties and I'd rip into
    them with my bare hands. Lift out the pink beef Frisbees and crack
    them apart on the counter and zing them into the broiler. I would have
    preferred to fry them, but HE wouldn't let me.

I'm the one responsible here.

I followed him out to the cellar one night. The ground was soft and
    uneven and I almost lost him. But I found him again.
With my mouth.
I kissed him, not knowing I was going to do it until I was already doing it.
    His mouth was cool and closed at first, and then it grew it opened and I
    thought, of course, about flowers.
And then, out of nowhere, the smell of roses, invisible.
Who planted these flowers? I knew they couldn't be wild.
I almost fell. I put my arms around him, but he kept his arms folded to his
    chest.
"Careful," he said.
I noticed his arms were full of tomatoes.
"Easy. These tomatoes are from my mother's garden."

*She tosses her composition book to the floor, leans forward and
speaks to the audience.*

I think we should start now.

11

She turns and looks at the vase on the end table. She's annoyed by it. She grabs the flowers out of the vase and tosses them carelessly upstage, then takes a long slow drink of the water from the vase. The following section is directed at specific members of the audience. If performed in some fancy-schmancy sort of theatre, you know, with c proscenium and real lights, not clamp lamps, which is quite unlikely, but in case it should happen, the performer addresses imaginary people in the audience. That's acting.

Did you have enough to eat?

How did you sleep? I'm sorry I got in bed with you. It was an accident. It used to be my bed. You kept on dreaming, I'm glad.

Should we lock up then? I don't think I have a key.

Should we leave a light on?

Did you go down to the water one last time?

What did I leave behind? I always leave something behind. I just don't know what it's going to be this time.

I can't tell you how happy I am you decided to come with me.

But this is where we split up.

You have to follow me. Take the red car.

I should have made a map. Do you mind getting lost?

I'll tell you what we can do. I can describe the important landmarks so that when we go by them you'll know—we *are* on the right track.

She walks upstage, talking.

So we'll head out about two miles north, out the Dixie Highway.

The first thing you'll notice on your right is a Denny's.

She turns downstage.

Not just any Denny's! This is the very same Denny's where I used to have dinner with my mother on my father's golf nights.

She sees the Denny's, floating somewhere just over the heads of the audience.

Oh my God! There we are!

Hunched over the menus, lost in the smell of fresh formica, potato salad,
and things in general frying.
My mother straightens her bifocals, she folds up her menu:
"I want to ask you a question, young lady. Do you like
boys
or girls
or both."

She giggles nervously. But I guess that's really the only way anyone giggles.

I lean forward, my nipples grazing the shrimp in a basket:
"Both," I said. "I like both."
"Well no wonder you can't hold down a full-time job," my mother says.
And the waitress overhears! She swoops down, apologizing, cocktail
sauce in one hand, tartar sauce in the other:
"Oh forgive me, I should have asked! You can have both! Here you go, help
yourself!"

And we'll pass by Apple Mountain.
It's not really a mountain. It's a pile of landfill they seeded over with a few
diseased elms. I know what you're thinking. You're thinking it's really
tacky to have a mountain made of garbage.
Well, you say that now, but you're new to Michigan, you live here as long
as I have you'll crave any kind of mountain you can get your hands on!
There's a little too much sky out here.
This is my favorite mountain because I went riding here when I was two.
I know I was two, I had to be two because my grandfather took me and
he was dead by the time I was three.

There must have been some kind of remission.

It was September, late. The light was something you could taste.
He walked ahead, his cane clobbering the goldenrod, the Queen Anne's
lace. He picked me up and put me on his horse. I wasn't afraid.

I was two inches from the sun.
I can still feel it.
The slow curve of the earth, a dying man's hands on my body, seven
hundred pounds of palomino between my legs.
Let me feel it again.

"Giddy-up!" I moved, the horse moved, the earth moved. Separately.

She addresses a member of the audience at point-blank range.

Do you realize the entire solar system is moving twelve miles a second
   towards the constellation Hercules?
Is that news to you? I knew it the first time I touched you. Back then I
   laughed. I asked him to take my shirt off. I thought I would never fall.

If you're hungry we can stop. Really. I wouldn't mind. I know a place. A
   great place. The H&H Bakery in Pinconning.
I used to think it was named after me.
So did my sister. She didn't care for the place.
I stopped there with my sister, my mother, two friends of mine.

Where was my father?
My mother was being so nice to me I didn't recognize her. She let us sit in
   a booth. She let us order milkshakes. She even promised to take us to—
   DEER ACRES!
Then, out of the woods, a porcupine started waddling across the parking
   lot.
"Look girls! A porkie!"
My mother called porcupines "porkies" and skunks she called—wood
   pussies.
"You wait right here." And Mom dashed out to the Buick and popped open
   the trunk.
And she lifted out an axe.

Porcupines have no natural enemies. Nothing in the world wants a
   mouthful of quills and the porcupines know this. They don't even know
   how to run.
Unfortunately.
I don't know how many times she must have hit the damn thing. Long
   after it was dead.
Maybe somebody in the restaurant kept count. They were all looking.
Then my mother came back into the restaurant, her hands were full of
   bloody flesh and quills. "Here you are, girls. Something for your class.
   Science!"
It could have been worse. It could have been a lot worse.
She put down the axe.

If you look quick, you'll see the house I grew up in, the house she almost died in. The day the ambulance came it was hot but her hands were ice. She was just lying there, moaning, little x's where the eyes should be. You know, like in a cartoon. It was . . . funny.

When the paramedics came into the room she started fussing with her bedclothes, she ran a blue hand through her hair. She opened her eyes.

"Are you going to check me out?" she said to the tallest.

I couldn't believe it! My mother was flirting on her deathbed. I hadn't seen her that frisky in a year.

They took her vital signs then they asked to see me in the hall.

Where was my father?

"Your mother's very sick."

"I know that. That's why she needs to go to a hospital."

"No she doesn't. Not anymore."

I went back into the room. I bent over her. The last of the peonies lay facedown in the dirt. I could hear the men waiting in the hall. I could smell them wanting a cigarette.

"Holly," she said. "Holly."

"Did you check out the tall guy? What a set of BUNS on that guy! I could almost taste them. I can't do anything about it, but you could."

Then the paramedics came back into the room and my mother turned to the tallest one and asked: "Why don't you just pick me up?"

And he did.

That's how she went out of the house the last time, in the arms of the ambulance man, talking dirty to him in her emphysemic wheeze. Her voice was like stale air forced through a bellows one last time.

I was the fire she fanned.

She sits down again in the armchair.

Just for the record, he did have a nice set of buns. But that's another story.

Pause. She leans back into the chair. She's home.

Here we are!

This is my land. It used to be my mother's land.

What am I saying? This still is my mother's land.

In this house, my mother refuses to sleep. She prefers to watch me sleep.
In the eyes of my mother, I sleep the way a blind woman swims under-
water. If she weren't still whispering in my ear, I don't think I'd ever
wake up.
Wait here.
I'll open the door.

*Blackout. She begins speaking into a microphone, whispering. As she
speaks, the lights ghost up excruciatingly slowly. By the end of this
section, the lights should be half up. Her manner is tender as though
speaking to a frightened child.*

Sssh. Listen to me, listen to me.
Was that you crying? Yes, it was. Don't lie to me.
Don't you think I'd know your cry by now?
In here, in the dark, alone. Like a baby.
Whose baby are you anyway? Huh?
Look at me. I'm just like you. I used to be a baby. I was scared.
Everybody's scared and nobody's scared enough.
Ssssh.
There's something I've got to tell you.
I don't have anything on underneath. Sssssh.

I sleep in the big bed all by myself. It's dangerous, I know. I could drown.
On the other hand, I can really spread out, take up all the space I want.
Like Africa. People see me on the street in the daytime and they think:
"What a small woman. You would be afraid of her?"
But they haven't been to bed with me. What do they know about fear?
At night, in bed, I'm a really tall woman for my size. I remember the
first time I came to this bed, the first time I saw Africa. I had on a really
good pair of boots. Talk about animals! Back then there were animals
as far as the eye could see, right in this very bed. I wasn't afraid. I was
hungry. I was very eager to get at least one pelt from every species. Not
like now! Everything I touch these days is turning into Europe on me.
Even this bed.

But this is MY bed. I said: "Let that man come to my bed with his guns out
like that, let him take whatever he wants from me, there's plenty more.
There's a lot more to me than he can kill. He's just a man. He used to be
a baby! He's afraid of me."

With good reason.

I am a continent. Trees grow through me. Trees whose roots go all the way to the other side of the world where they bloom as roses, peace roses, tea roses, roses named after all the dead Presidents and their mistresses. All these roses. Where do they come from? Right out of the top of my head. I made them up!

So could you. We're both the same. We're both full of roses.

We need rain, don't we?

I don't remember why.

I am raining. I am the rain.

I don't remember why.

I'm nobody's baby.

She opens her eyes but doesn't look at anyone yet. She takes a long drink from the vase as the lights slowly crossfade up to a more general, brighter level. There is a sense of waking up. Of coming "to." Gee, I hope that doesn't sound too hokey. I think it works.

All I really wanted from my mother was her French.

The woman leans back in the chair and closes her eyes. From offstage left comes the faint sounds of an accordion. I'd really prefer a set of bagpipes, but the accordion is more reasonable. The song is sweet, like a remembered childhood song, something upbeat, por favor. The woman smiles, the song is part of her reverie. Suddenly, her eyes open. She realizes the song is not part of the dream, but is really happening. A woman enters playing the accordion. She is tall, with broad shoulders and good bones, elegant and eccentric—a midwestern Marlene Dietrich, let's say. She's wearing a smoking jacket and very little else other than the accordion. She reminds you of those Saturday mornings when your dad would dress up like Clark Gable and chase your mother around the breakfast nook with his semiannual hard-on. As the song progresses, the woman in the chair relaxes and dives back into her dream. She speaks as though she's dictating a letter into a foreign language, one she barely knows.

I'd say . . . Oh, Mama, I can't sleep at night. I smell the ocean. Not that far-off Atlantic, not the unbelievable Pacific. I'm talking about that old ocean, that blue blanket that used to cover this country, all of us, from the teenage anorexics to the Burger King evangelists, all of us sleeping with the dinosaurs, the black-capped chickadees, our heads full of fish, waiting to be born.

That's the ocean that floods my bed each night and what can I do about it, Mama?

I get up in the morning and the world is just flat and dry and there is no hint, in the parking lot, at the mall, at the 7–Eleven, of why I am so full of ocean. Do you know what I saw?

I saw a boy grab a cat and sit on it and pee all over it. I saw a man hit his wife so hard the whole house cried, I swear. The big blue Colonial was weeping to see this woman down on her hands and knees, picking up the three-bean salad, picking it up, bean by bean.

All I want to do is sleep, Mama. I'm just like everybody else.

But I'm sinking, I'm turning to stone because of what I saw that night: that woman's blood and tears on the dining-room shag, snaking out of her, spelling out curses in a language NOT English. She was saying: "I'm sorry, I'm sorry," but her blood was singing another tune. It was singing . . .

Sorrow. Death. Death to all of us in this woman's tears. Mama, am I the only one who can read tears?

Oh, I can't watch TV anymore, I can't watch TV. There's always some guy on TV laughing and everyone is laughing with him, except for this woman and me. I know she's gonna cry enough in the next week to flood us all out of our houses, even the ones who are laughing.

Am I the only one who's afraid of drowning?

Teach me to swim, Mama! Teach me how to read this sorrow so I can resist the common current. Mama, teach me that French!

Mama says, "What makes you think I know any French?" Her voice is cool and blind, but, and this is a big but, she puts her hand on her hips and I see those hips move under her wraparound skirt so heavy and full, I can smell the memory of ocean drifting out from between her legs. Oh there is *power* in my mother's hips! I tell you what I've seen! I've seen her hands with their tapered fingers run from her hips down to her thighs, I've seen her tongue sneak out of her mouth to wet her lips when everyone else was just watching TV and I know, oh, yes, I know, my mother is *full* of *French.*

The two of us? Two of a kind. She gets up when the rest of us are sleeping to do a slow and sultry striptease for her private audience of African violets and oh! How they bloom. And me? Well, the thing you got to remember about me is I was born feet first, that's right, after forty years of living inside her I came out of her feet first, wearing this dress, high heels and this bracelet. I guess you could say I was *born* to speak French.

Mama took me to the bathroom and started asking me questions. Taking off her clothes and asking me questions. With every garment I got a new question. She unbuttons her blouse and asks: "Do you want to know where babies come from?" She shimmies out of her skirt and says: "Are you ready for the meaning of life? I'm talking about the secret life, the French nightclub where we're all dancing? The hidden room where we stash our gold." She says this and VOILA!

My mother's got no underwear on. Her pantyhose . . . it's down there on the ground, sulking, feeling sorry for himself, then that old pantyhose just slinks on out of there, belly to the ground. And my mother is standing in front of me . . . *(She mimes to the audience)* NAKED. Uh-HUH. NA-KED. And glistening. Bigger than life, shining from the inside out, just like that giant jumbo Rhode Island Red Hen in front of the Chicken Palace and Riborama.

> *The woman's attitude is extremely important throughout this section beginning with the strip in the bathroom. Her tone should be one of an initiate witnessing a sacred ritual, a mystery revealed. The tone is awe, which can be misinterpreted as fear and lead to a reading of this passage as an incestual event. But no matter what a girl does, there will be those nuevo puritans among us who see something dirty in this. I suggest they read Joe Campbell or the Great Mother, hell, even the* World Book *probably talks about "Fertility Rites." See it's all in the classics.*

And she's smelling of salt, and she's promising me grease, something to suck on, and she's asking me in, oh, she's asking me in. And my legs are trembling, just like a diver's legs, because I'm high above that sweet pink ocean, that body of water that is a body, the body we call Mother, and I'm about to go in. Oh, I'm about to go in.

Mama says: "Holly, if something's bothering you, and you want to know the answer to it, just remember the answer is inside you." And with that she reached inside herself and then she took her hand out and oh! I could see how wet she was! And that smell! Let me tell you about that smell! That smell made me want to do the mashed potato! Just me and my mother, my naked mother, dancing in the split-level.

She said she liked to smell herself. She liked to see herself open to nothing but her own eyes. It made her a better gardener. It's true. It's like her purple lips gave her a certain sympathy for the tomatoes. She could get them to go red when everybody else had a yard full of little green fists of fruit. She knew she was a tomato. Crawling through the mud. Or a rose, trained to climb up the sides of houses.

She said: "Holly, I know you're afraid of the world, and with good reason. My father was a trout fisherman! And what did he use for bait? Mice. *Live* mice. He'd chop off their legs and tie them to a hook and oh! They were so attractive before they drowned! That's what fish like. And I started to beg for those fish, those were my favorite fish. That's what's scary. I know you're afraid of the world and with good reason. But Holly, this is your clitoris, let me tell you what she does for a living! It doesn't do any good to be afraid of the world!"

> *The woman with accordion quickly picks up the pace, and the alleged performer dances around the set. Something waltzy, but the kind of waltz you'd do in a dress from Frederick's of Hollywood. The performer speaks as she flops back down in the chair.*

That's what we call "using the space."

Years later I'm in school and I'm trying to learn everybody else's French and I'm saving my milk money, working on a hunch there's going to be some sort of palomino in my future, when I discover a big problem. I'm telling the story I just told you to my best friend at the time, Jo-deen *Windy* Thompson, and all of sudden, she's looking at me funny, like I'm bleeding or something. Like seeing my mother's pussy is some sort of crime. And so I have to tell her that's not the way I saw it. To me it was a gift. It was the best thing she ever did for me. It was my inheritance.

And Jo-deen *Windy* Thompson said: "If it was so damn good how come you're crying?" And I said: "Jo-deen *Windy* Thompson, you know damn well I spent my entire childhood in church, trying to see Jesus. And I never did see him! But now I finally did! I saw Jesus between my mother's legs! And when you see Jesus, you're gonna cry, too!"

Do you know what she said? She said: "Holly, my mother does NOT have a pussy and if she did, I wouldn't want to know about it!"

Well! Am I surprised? No! It's no wonder she can't grow jackshit in that tired old garden of theirs. Her mother couldn't keep a cactus wet. Oh, but you got to feel sorry for them. Her mother's got that rotten brown color of hair. They're just a couple of roses forced to bloom underground.

What if the worst is true? Do you ever think, what if the worst is true? Do you know what that would mean? That would mean the born-agains and the feminists are BOTH RIGHT.

Hmmm.

That would mean the birthplace of sin IS seeing that your mother's got a pussy and knows what to do with it. That would make my mother just a snake in housewife's clothing, and that apple she's offering me a poison apple. But do you know what? I'd bite anyway, I'd bite today. Because I would rather know what a snake knows than grow up to be Jo-deen *Windy* Thompson, doomed to drown in her own body, doomed to wear her body like it's somebody else's clothes, doomed to die never realizing her mother's got anything other than Astroturf between her legs, miniature golf, hole in one.

Oh the things they teach you in school. I discover big problem number two. You see the French I got from my mother, and the French they're trying to teach me in school—they don't match.

They're saying my mother did not know French. That this way of talking with her tears and her pussy and with her sentences which could say "Death" but mean "Pleasure" at the same time, and her words, her words which were like fifteen gold bracelets sliding down the arm of a woman dancing in a French nightclub—they're saying that's NOT French! None of this is the real French. None of what was said between us was real at all.

Oh the things they teach you in school. Do you know what I learned in school? There's no word in French or any other language for the kind of woman my mother was, no word for a woman who was a woman and a mother at the same time, no word for a woman who had that kind of power over tomatoes. But I swear, I saw it happen.

Or did I make it all up?

How about that time she was out of the house and I'm there with my friend, Richard Goodsell, and oh! He is one skinny thing. He's funny and smart but he's too bony and nervous to have any other friends but me. His fingers are always bloody from sawing away at that damn violin, night and day. Well so Richard is getting the shit beaten out of him, pardon my French, on a regular basis, and so I have to go to bed with him.

Oh don't get me wrong! I like Richard, but it's not like I want to do anything with his thing, besides, we're ten and there's not much of a thing in the first place. I like Richard in that animal sort of way. They won't let the horses be alone in the barn! Not the best horses! You have to have another body in there, in the dark. So this time, when Richard gets the shit beaten out of him, pardon my French, I get right on top of him, I try to iron the tears out of that scrawny bag of bones. And all of a sudden my mother's home and she tries to pull me off him but I fight, oh I fight just like a horse going out of a burning building! Because sometimes, you don't know why, but you just got to go up in *flames*!

And my mother's screaming: "What are you doing!"
And I'm screaming: "You don't understand!"
But I look at her. She's crying. I don't understand. Because my mother is
    crying: "I don't want you to be like me! I don't want them to do to you
    what they did to me!"

Okay. That was the time I stopped seeing my mother as a woman who invented her own language, one where she was the engine inside every verb she had. She stopped looking like a magician. She looked like a liar. Do you know what they said about my mother? They said: "Holly, your mother is crazy. Nobody did anything to her. She's just crazy." And I started to agree. Little while later, we were both right. My mother was one crazy bitch.

Shortly thereafter I went to art school.

> *Music up, loud, dance music, French Bobby Darin sort of stuff. The performer howls. The accordion player puts down her instrument, grabs a mike and begins singing in her best faux French. The performer dances around—wild, ebullient, terrible dance. The song is sometimes called "Viva Lawn Chair" and is basically nonsense punctuated with some real words such as "ratatouille," "Chevrolet," "coupe de ville," "Jacques Cousteau" and "Kalamazoo." When they and the audience are exhausted, the singer dips the performer, and exits through the audience. The performer collapses in the chair.*

Oh I cannot tell a lie. If you came to see lies you're out of luck. Oh I tried to learn how to lie, in art school, and I learned to believe in the universality of art, that art transcends the grubby artless ghettos of gender and race and sexual preference, that art is abstract and never gets blood on his clothes even when witnessing a murder, oh, no! Art turns the other way and looks out the window. And even though I can parlez-vous with the best of them, even though I know how to lie by abstraction, allusion, irony, inference (Oh! The tools of modern art are at my disposal, they are at the disposal of me!), my mother's invented French is stronger. It just keeps bleeding through all that art-school training.

I just can't keep my mother's French out of my artwork.

And I can't shut out the deaths of Lisa Steinberg and the witch trial of her stepmother and the death of Jennifer Levin and all the other deaths I feel inside but I don't have their names. I don't have their names because the women were too dark or old or poor or queer or hot to even get seen with the naked eye of journalism, forget about art. Hey, I know this is ruining my artwork and it's not getting me any new boyfriends, I'll tell you that. (This is the first time since I came out that I'm having a real shortage of boyfriends.) I'm getting too crazy to be an artist much longer. I just can't tell a lie much longer.

On the bus uptown the other day two black men in work clothes are sitting across from me and the one guy says: "White people are killing me." And his friend says: "I know." Then he says: "They hate us so much they don't even know they are doing it. They hate us, but we're supposed to like them. If you hate them, you're crazy." His friend says: "I know."

The man says: "They say they don't hate blacks but look who they put in the White House, and I do mean the *White* House." His friend says: "I know." Then this man says: "I hate them. I hate their women, I hate their children. Those stupid little white babies! Have you ever noticed how many *white* people are having babies these days?"

I cannot tell a lie. I always like it when someone who's black is nice to me. It helps me forget, for a moment, that I'm a member of the DAR. My mother signed me up. She said: "I know how much you like those women's organizations."

When someone who is black is nice to me I forget for a moment that I am descended from a long line of women who had elaborate gardens and plenty of domestic help. Women who, smiling, bent over each evening from a great height to feed the terriers and the black women. It doesn't have anything to do with me, does it? I'm not racist. It's all in the past, right.

Right?

Well, I do like dogs. I like dogs to lick my hands. Helps me forget about all the species we've wiped out.

Oh I cannot tell a lie, I'm hated and I return the sentiment because it's just too big for art and I'm too old for abstraction. I think I feel okay about saying this because we're all women here tonight, right? Okay. We're not all women. But we're all lesbians. I mean anyone can be a lesbian, gender is no obstacle.

Giggling. She is sweet and intimate during this section.

Men just kill me. They really do. They are killing us. They hate us women so deep and hard they don't even know they're doing it. They say: "I like women, I'm all for equal rights!"

But what's this antiabortion fever gripping the nation, huh?

What's this unending lack of funding for the children they cared so much about as fetuses, then abandoned as children? Oh, I know what you're thinking. You're thinking there's women in the antiabortion movement. Well, that's what they *want* you to think! Those are not *women.* Nancy Reagan isn't even human, she's a hand puppet.

And what about one of my other favorite cocktail-party conversation topics—battered women. You know what I read in the paper the other day about battered women? "If they don't like it, why don't they leave? Hedda Nussbaum, she could have just left." But what I don't read is where are we supposed to go? Oh show me on a map, Mr. Señor Monsieur, Ms. Famous Feminist, where in the world can a woman walk?

Hedda Nussbaum did leave. Twice.

Oh, I know! This is not art! Believe you me, I wish I could be whipping out a haiku, or doing a little macramé demonstration—I wish I could be sharing some art with you right now. I'm just like everybody else. All I want to do is sleep.

Oh I know the difference between politics and art! I went to art school—I didn't say I graduated, but I did matriculate—and the first thing they said when they saw me coming through the door was: "Holly, don't hit them over the head. Art is not supposed to hit them over the head!"

Well neither are fathers. And when Joel Steinberg hit his daughter so hard she died I read in the paper the next day a columnist, Pete Hamill, saying it was worse morally for Hedda Nussbaum to not intervene than it was for Joel Steinberg to kill her in the first place. That's when I gave up on my macramé career.

Let me ask you a question. Take all the time you want. Here's something that's been bothering me lately. Why is it, if men don't hate women, like they claim that they don't, why do they ask such stupid questions, like "Where are all the great women artists?" Is that a question for me? You know where they are—they're out in the kitchen, for chrissakes, making you a fucking cup of coffee, okay?

I'm getting kind of hot under the collar and I don't even have a collar on!

Let me ask you another question, sort of in the same vein. If men don't hate women, why is it when I go to see a movie featuring my favorite movie star du jour, Jodie Foster, in that movie she made, *The Accused*, why was it that during the rape scene the men were cheering! I thought I was at the Rose Bowl. And why was it, when I went to see Almodóvar's *Matador*, during the rape scene, the men were laughing. Laughing. I'm thinking: "Do you think this is funny? If you think this is funny why don't

you get your ass down to a rape crisis center and man those hotlines."
And yes, I do mean *man* those hotlines.

Come to think of it, it's a bad idea. But you could go out for coffee. Or clean
up the bathroom. It's easy. Make sure there's plenty of fresh maxi-pads
and odor-eaters on hand.

What? Where's my sense of humor? You want to see my sense of humor?
Then drop your pants and bend over and I got ten hard inches of throb-
bing one-liners for you.

Oh men are killing me. And they want me to like them. You know, men
can laugh at rape, but if you say you hate them, you're crazy. I'm very
sorry, I don't like them. You see, I'm a man-hater.

Oh yes.

Of course, I don't hate men half as much as a straight woman would but
I'm still a man-hater. *(She's giggling as she says it)*

What's the matter here? Are you mad at me?

    She is as sincere as possible.

Are you gonna sit there and sulk. Are you gonna leave? So leave.
If you all leave I get to go home early.
Why don't you say what you really think about me. Just spit it out. I can
   take it. What's it going to be—whore! Slut?
That's very good. I am a whore, I am a slut.
If you get two choices, whore or good girl, I'll be a whore any day.
And here's something else: If I'm a whore that's what you like about me.
   And number two, I'm a whore for a very good reason, I'm good at it.
   Some people can sing, some people can dance and some of us just
   know how to fuck.

It's a gift. From God.

(Softly) Do you have any idea at all of how much I love you?
Do you think I would waste my breath on you if I didn't?
Look at me. I know you're afraid. I know that because I used to be a baby
   and I was scared.
But everybody's scared and nobody's scared enough.

But we did share a bed together. You remember that bed. Think of that bed and answer me—why is it if you love me, if you love me, if you love women, why was it after the rape you kept showing me picture after picture of black men when I told you once, a thousand times, it was a *white* man who raped me. And what did you say?

"It could have been worse."

Oh, just my luck.

Why was it, after the rape, you said: "Holly, you're lucky he came. If they don't come they like to kill."

Is that so?

Don't you know I slept with fifty men by the time I was eighteen, I didn't come with one of them, but I never thought about killing them.

But that could all change tonight. I could set a new policy! Get it right the first time or pay the big price, boyfriend!

Oh men are killing me. I know they're in pain, oh their pain is famous. But their pain is going to be the death of me. Their pain and their words. Saying they love me. Saying they love women. I don't think that's what they mean. I wish I did, but I don't. I think that what they mean is: "Boys will be boys."

Thank you very much, but I would rather be crazy.

About my words, when I say that I hate men, you have to understand that hate is the dark side of love.

Don't just take my word for it. Ask Mr. Freud.

But I'm not counting on you loving me back. I don't think you can hear what I'm saying. I might as well be speaking my private French.

She sits down. Takes a drink of water from the vase. Relaxes.

Well, I was probably crying. And a man came up to me, big guy. Looked familiar. When he told me his name I said, "Oh, well you knew my mother when she was young. What was she like?"

HOLLY HUGHES

And he said: "I liked your mother. All the men in Saginaw liked your
mother."

"She was pretty."

"Oh she was pretty all right! She was pretty unusual for a woman from
Saginaw. You know there used to be a word for the kind of woman your
mother was and it started with an *S*."

"Are you trying to tell me that my mother . . . liked to, ah . . . dance?"

"Oh, your mother liked to dance all right! She was a SHAMELESS
dancer."

I looked at this guy. I thought I should just spit in his face. I couldn't see
his face very well because it was covered by the shadow cast from his
oversize toupee. I should have spit anyway. I mean, it was her funeral.
But something stopped me.
I believed him when he said that he liked her. He didn't mean to say
anything bad about her.

After my mother died, seven blue herons flew right over the top of the
Holiday Inn and landed smack-dab in the middle of our front lawn.
Meaning . . . you tell me. And after my mother died I was having this
dream about my mother and she was drowning so I went in the water
after her. And she just kept swimming farther and farther out, saying it
was really silly for me to try to save her because I was the one who was
drowning. After my mother died, I probably don't have to tell you this, but
all of my sentences started with: "After my mother died . . . ." And then, a
little while after my mother died, the only thing I really wanted to do was
fuck.

So there's this guy at work, right. Jeez! Always hovering over my PC
asking me if I want to go to a Blarney Stone, right? So finally I said to
him: "Look, I hate you. You're an idiot. I'm a lesbian. You touch me,
you're a dead man, okay?"

And he's just laughing and laughing. I've never been so funny in all my
life.

After my mother died, I told him that she had died. And he started to cry, I
mean, he started to cry! I couldn't believe it. This idiot this dumbo I
had yelled at fifty times a day to get out of my face was crying all over
the copier about my mother.

And I thought: "Okay, sucker, maybe you're going to get lucky after all."

All of a sudden I knew what I wanted. I wanted to be nasty. I wanted to be

2 8

nasty in Spanish, because if you're going to do it you might as well do it in Spanish, it sounds better: "*Sin vergüenza.*" I wanted to be desnuda in my terrarium with this junior account executive from Middle Village Queens, I wanted to be outside of history, I wanted to rewrite the Bible, so I said "Let's go to the Blarney Stone." We went there and we knocked back a few pink squirrels.

Then I took him . . . downtown.

On the Lexington Avenue local he detailed the various disgusting acts he was going to commit to my defenseless body and then he asked what I had in store for him.

I said: "Okay, cowboy. Here's the program. You're on the menu. We're going to go for broke, we're going to take the plunge. I have plans to rewrite the Bible and when I get through with you tonight, this is the way it's going to read from now on."

She leans back in the chair. She slips into another world like she is slipping into a silk robe.

Oh! They were naked at last.
Cara a cara entre azul y buenas noches.
Face to face between blue and holy nights.
Two ficus trees, two alley cats, two ancient jade plants growing out of the same straw hat. You could call this a walk-up Garden of Eden. And the first word spoken is: "*Ooh-la-la.*"

I will translate.

This means they were naked and they knew it and they didn't care. They didn't care! They didn't care about the white trash across the air shaft, they didn't care about the Ukrainian ladies across St. Mark's Place with their raw elbows propping up opera glasses, they didn't care about the Blue Oyster Cult fans that lived downstairs from Eve who couldn't see them but might be able to hear the second words spoken which were: "*Ooh-la-la.*"

Adam begging Eve to sit on his face.

Well! By now Eve's fingers are galloping up and down Adam's fly and our heroine decides to treat Mr. Adam to a little seminar. So, she reaches out and grabs him where he lives, Italian style, and says: "Mr. Adam,

Querido Señor, God has sure lied to you! You're not the first man. You're just the first man this month, ooh-la-la! And that sound of zippers, *¡escuche!* It's holy. You can hear the word of God in it. Jesus loves us, even though he hasn't been invented yet. Jesus loves you, Mr. Adam and those luscious polycotton Sansabelt pants with the delicious Velcro tabs because Jesus loves that getting naked sound almost as much as you my tits. Yes, I know they're perfect. They came in the mail, just last week from the Fruit of the Month Club!
On the other hand, it could be they didn't exist at all until you started sucking on them.

And Mr. Adam, what is the meaning of that business I see leaning out of your pants like that! I haven't seen anything that ah . . . interesting since my last trip to the Vatican!

And Mr. Adam, aqui esta la pregunta du jour:
Where in the world do you want to do the monkey business?
Anything is possible as long as you remember:
We are the sons and daughters of meat. We are barely descended from mud. This is the start of history, starting with my hand, wet, on your wet dick.

Which is wetter, Adam or Eve? Which is closer to the sea?

And Adam says, "I don't know, baby, let's just do it against the wall."

And he presses her against the wall and he spreads her legs like a like a . . . ah . . . I don't know. Like nothing else could. Because, recuerda, this is the beginning, beginning with Mr. Adam sliding in his cock slow, very slow, a little bit too slow for this heroine but you got to remember this is a work of fiction!

And this is an unusual part in the narrative, in fact in my entire oeuvre, because it's where I admit I might be wrong. Maybe I was wrong. Maybe Mr. Adam is no Dumbo after all. He knows shame didn't just ram its way into the newborn human mind, oh no. Tragedy takes time! More time and care than the sixteen thrusts average for average heterosexual coitus. (According to condom research. Just one of those things I know.)

Adam is happy, Eve is happy. They're both happy there's Sheetrock surrounding this Garden of Eden. And then Mr. Adam is very happy because he's all the way inside her and he can feel her feel him hit . . . Pay Dirt.

All of a sudden, Eve has just *got* to say: "Yo! Buddy! Do you know who I am? Do you have any idea at all who you are porking? I'm the preeminent lesbian performance artist from southern Michigan."

And all Mr. Adam's got to say is: "Hot damn, baby, all I know about you is how wet you are." He gives it to our heroine a little harder and asks her if she has any hobbies.

This is one of them.

Eve doesn't say anything about her other . . . hobbies. Eve doesn't say nada about nada, because, praise the Lord, words fail her. She can see her mother dancing in Dayton. She can see herself on the outside of history where todo el mundo se habla español.

I'm going to translate.

That means where everyone is shirtless, shiftless, good for nothing but being bad . . . "sin vergüenza."

> *She crosses to the vase, takes a drink. Picks up her notebook and turns around to speak to the audience directly, but softly.*

When you think of me, why don't you just eat an apple.

Chew very carefully, I am still your apple. Lick every drop of juice that drips down your chin and say: "Help me. I want to change. Let me be changed."

It could happen. Didn't it happen at least once?

Didn't it happen that night I held you and I ate you until your singing golden skin was all the way inside me? Weren't you changed then? Weren't you an apple then?

It's not always February. We don't always drink this weak tea.

Even for my father and my mother, there was a late August.

When she got sick he took very good care of her. He could understand her at last, she was like work to him.

See my mother on the last night of her life? My father bends over the scrawny bed. I could see the bones in his face for the first time. He feels like a farmer towards her. "Help me," she says.

And he does. He kisses her.

Not gently. Her mouth is open and I see her tongue.

Apples are suddenly everywhere! The fly is out of the amber, the teapot boils down in the western sky. Help me, I am dying to change.

She pulls him on top of her. His hand goes between her legs. On the last night of my mother's life my father's hand is red. Red! Red from the light of apples falling. Suddenly apples fall like rain outside the bedroom window.

Oh. I get it. After she's gone we'll still have pie.

And now I see my mother touch my father. I see him shimmy. I see him change. I see him, oh I see him.

He is an apple in her hands.

    Exit. Blackout.

THE FATHER

BEATRICE ROTH

BEATRICE ROTH

Beatrice Roth, the daughter of a Jewish storekeeper who wanted to be a farmer, was born in the predominantly Protestant town of Northampton, Pennsylvania in 1919. She is the oldest of seven children and has two daughters.

Although she left her hometown when she was twenty-one to become an actress in New York, her family and early life have been the major source for Roth's solo performances. She sets this material in the larger framework of metaphors from nature. In *Seventeen* she recalls the year of her mother's death, "a year of personal upheaval, an indelible year," placing it in a metaphorical context "of the geologic evolvement of the earth." In *At That Time I Was Studying Carole Lombard* she draws parallels between her adolescent fantasies and the glittering lives of movie stars, with their promise of glamour and romance. It is about "cultural sculpting getting in the way of the growth of a young woman, or influencing her personal growth. I put that in the context of the grandeur, the destiny of sequoia trees." For *The Father*, which addresses "a very isolated religious structure which gets broken up by events that are disordering," she uses the metaphor of rocks broken up into "the indestructability of sand."

Roth was a professional actress for more than fifteen years, from the early forties to the late sixties. She trained with Stella Adler, was a member of the Actors Studio, and played in stock, Off and on Broadway, and in television. But the available roles were often unfulfilling.

> There wasn't enough Chekhov or anything else I liked to do. So I left traditional theatre and I didn't think I would act again, I was painting and going through all the turmoils of life and then I began to see some experimental work and I was very excited by it.

In a workshop at the School for Movement Research Roth developed her first solo work, *Cave Woman,* a movement piece without words. She developed some of her subsequent solos at the ReCherChez studio, getting feedback from Ruth Maleczech and Lee Breuer of Mabou Mines, and has been part of Wooster Group projects.

Roth's performances are distinguished by her skillfulness as an actor and her delicate, birdlike physicality. Her style is elegant and feminine; although her age gives her an air of fragility, she projects a self that is sexual, playful and passionate. As Irina in the Wooster Group's work-in-progress, which uses material from Chekhov's *Three Sisters,* she is a remarkably convincing young girl.

In her performances Roth frequently uses simple props that have metaphoric or symbolic significance. For *The Father* she wears her father's prayer shawl and pours sand, occasionally introducing the sound of dovening, or praying. In her recent work, the visual settings have become more elaborate, involving filmed animation, slides, video.

Beatrice Roth's The Father *premiered at New York's Performing Garage in 1985, as the third part of* Trilogy. *She has performed the piece all over the New York area, as well as in Minneapolis, Boston and Providence, and in Pennsylvania and New Hampshire. The first part of the trilogy,* Seventeen, *was published in* The Massachusetts Review *(Spring 1983).* At That Time I Was Studying Carole Lombard *is the trilogy's middle section.*

THE FATHER

In the dimness she starts a tape in her Walkman. It is the rich passion-
ate voice of a Jew singing his morning prayers in the privacy of his
home. She rearranges the table in front of her with a few objects
suggesting a Sabbath setting: a bottle of wine and goblet, a seashell
covered with linen, a geode, a knife, a small blackened silver salt
cellar, a peanut-butter jar filled with sand, a crystal urn with cover.
This ceremony completed, she lowers the volume of the tape and leans
in to it to hear more intimately. Her first lines alternate with the lines
of the man singing, as if she were translating them.

He thought she would never actually leave home.
Yet when she did he visited arriving early on the Sunday excursion
in time to take her out to a hot breakfast.
The father believed in hot cereal.
She believed in chance.

She turns off the tape, places the Walkman on the floor and pours the
wine.

For years after she left the father's house
she wakened still to the echo of his dovening
the father prayed an hour and a half each morning
his totality wrapped in stripe and fringe
his forehead strapped in leather ribbon
his consciousness trapped in holy cube containing sacred parchment
covering his third eye.
He fed the pet canary while he dovened.

His murmur-song-secrets with his God seep into their final dream-
   state.
Woke and washed tumbling to their breakfast all that remained
was the cold air from the open-and-shut of his departure.
Working early   worrying late
dinner was at noon everyone walked home he gulped his food and
   washed his mouth and rushed back to the store
head a-tilt
arms a-swing   unevenly
favoring the work-worn topography of his frame
was tall and dark and disappearing
his presence in the house a rarity   a scarity
his absence a stern
turning on the Sabbath fleshly
fingers dipping honey
thawing all the week's denials.
His teeth were small and perfect
he had them all upon his death
of course he was only sixty when he died
still in those days if you had all your teeth at sixty . . .

He wore a half-smile always when he dovened
that is how she came to memorize his teeth.
His intimacy was with his God.
It was the only intimacy discernible until
one day on a Sabbath as it happened
she was summoned
running in the corridor rounding the square corner
entering standing watching waiting
in he strides fresh from synagogue
his gaze bent on the silken maze
he bends
and with practiced certainty
cups and kisses
drinking drowning flooding every bone and hollow
natural so natural
the shock is thunderous.
In the corner
in the shadows

in her dark and watchful cornea
lightning strikes splitting vision
illumining

> Something ontological
> no such fissure in her
> claustrophobic distance
> with the mother

Bent above the open pine box
his arms about the tiny brothers
peppering the powdery gravel
he is sprinkling on the purpling cheeks

> burying with her
> in the ground
> their secret

She raises the geode as if to strike, but stops and moves to the rug and places the geode on it. Squatting by it, she speaks.

Even the hardest rock shatters
sometimes suddenly as in a rockslide
sometimes slowly as by the cadence of a waterfall
inevitably
begins the journey.
The journey's made by rain and river
delays along the way
stuck in sediment of flood
re-routed by the wind
clasped in glacial frivolity
delays as on any trip
sometimes up to a million years
inevitably released
by frost and wind
to complete the ordained pilgrimage

> to check in at last upon the beach

She returns to chair, stands behind it and sweeps her bright magenta shawl to the floor. Beneath it is a prayer shawl.

When the mother died the father broke down and became sensual.

    She sits.

First with headaches

                        skipping days at the store

then with touching

                        his hands uncurled

then with softening

                        his face fell

                        into curves

he fell
in love

                        with his brother's wife

She may have loved him too.
She may have loved him all along.
Sure.
Vain though she was it was not all vanity responding to his affection.

                        Firstly she came on.

She came on cooking serving until things could settle

                        she was warm

                        compassionate

                        there

she preferred being there her husband Abraham and she were not affec-
tionate that anyone could see Abraham was brusque proud of her she
was good-looking

                        Being fat was no deterrent

                        those days in their culture

                        being thin was somewhat

                        suspect

not having enough
not having eaten enough perhaps

The youngest sisters part and comb his hair.
They hover giggle fuss and joke with him.
He touches women in their presence
arm about leaning in hair mingling
this could be a comfort

a relief

a girl of seventeen full of her own sense

and incense

her own pursuits
on the brink

Go

Plunge

. . . ohhh . . .

She breathes a path around the rim circumventing
choosing pink ground clasping red flowers to her belly

swaying slender

up against the satin cutting board
stuffing tarts
fashioning Daddy's darling favorite honey cake
chopping daydreams with the onions
grinding passion with the pepper
paring jealousy wafer thin with the

stainless steel stiletto

stealing to the castle to the portals
of her unsuspecting fairy princess

pointing
jabbing
stabbing

to her very corsets staining
her *own* ardent and rebellious landscape.   No
this is not a movie
Her *own*   ardent   and   rebellious   and   o

bedient
puritan
waspish jewish Cinderella

*Treating the shell as bread, she takes up the knife and salt cellar, and
performs the breaking-bread ceremony, chanting lines as the accompanying prayer.*

He thought she would never actually

leave home

Yet when she did

he came to her performance

41

Following one as Joan

                                    of Arc

Concerned

                                    she asked him

Daddy

how was it seeing me wear a cross on my knees to saints and deities

                                    he himself did not revere

                                    she watched him

think watched his heart bend toward her

at last he spoke

   She lifts the shell, shaking it gently before her eyes.

But that was Joan's belief

                                    was it not . . .

   To the shell, holding it still now.

I want to know you.

How you survived your birth found food how you multiplied stood up to

your first there-is-no-turning-back

how you recognized your enemies

how you surpassed your melancholy

   She slowly pours the sand from the peanut-butter jar into the crystal
   urn.

In a strange bed in a hospital in a strange city

brought for one of medicine's more arrogant experiments

they vigil with him.

One August afternoon she and he alone receive a local rabbi

sent for to say Tilim with him. The rabbi stands beside the bed

small next to the outstretched fingers held rigid by a needle conducting

glucose through a transparent tube attached to a pouch above the bed.

The rabbi stands

a stranger here to perform an act of intimacy.

The father's smile quavers firmly

to put the stranger at his ease.

It goes unanswered.

The glucose persists shimmying downward pressing the reluctant vein.
The litany begins.
The rabbi's voice is thin.
The father's unwavering in its wavering.
The rabbi's words inaudible, eyes lidded by embarrassment.
The father bypasses this licensed emissary
his voice a feather each strand articulate faintness.
Suddenly the transparent tube shudders.
The glucose shimmies backward up the tube defying gravity.
That other tube leading from a fading intellect is lit by a beam begun
aeons earlier—a flash so dazzling, the vein spits the unnatural fluid
back into its desperate channel.
The father's eyes burn black.
Singed by a current
propelling his spirit.

Days later hurried break for sandwich luncheon
detained by table service busy harassed waitress
brother-in-law chiding sister for her sadness
rush back stand a moment in the doorway
he is asleep.
One step takes you to his side.
Kiss his forehead.
It is warm

> remains warm for your kiss
> though he is far beyond

Bent over
your brother stands sobbing in the bathroom.
Bent over
your brother is bleeding on a Korean field.

She lets the sand run out in silence. Replaces lids on jar and urn,
begins to scrape cloth clean of sand.

On holy days and on the Sabbath he reclined at table and while chanting
the after-dinner gratitude he scraped and gathered every crumb and
morsel until his place became immaculate. Next morning wrapped in
stripe and fringe depending on the weather he flung wide the screen or
raised the pane a crack to scatter last night's breadcrumbs among the

gathered, feathered congregation. Of all that I recall I sometimes think this may be what I miss most—

She breaks off suddenly. Swiftly, but distinctly aware of each, she piles the objects used earlier in the trilogy from the floor onto the table. Now the floor around her is clear. With magenta shawl in hand she is about to leave—a split second and she adds the shawl to the pile, and walks out the way she came in. Lights out.

FROM
UNITED
STATES

LAURIE
ANDERSON

LAURIE ANDERSON

Laurie Anderson, the first daughter and second child in a family of eight children, was born in Chicago in 1947 and raised in northern Illinois, where her father was in the house-paint business and her mother trained horses. Her interest in telling fanciful tales emerged around the family dinner table, where a good story won attention.

At Mills College in California, where she went because it was far away, Anderson studied pre-med. She preferred doing the drawings for her classes to the research, and didn't like the school: "We had to wear long dresses to Wednesday-night dinner." She transferred to Barnard and after graduating with a major in art history, did sculpture for a year, studying with Sol LeWitt and Carl Andre at the School of Visual Arts before getting her MFA from Columbia. In the early seventies Anderson lectured on Egyptian architecture and Assyrian sculpture at City College, where she sometimes stretched the facts to make them more interesting. "I realized I like being in dark rooms with people. The teaching led to performing."

Anderson's offbeat sense of humor and penchant for social criticism and exaggerating the stories she tells fits in with her view of herself as being in the tradition of Mark Twain and William Burroughs. Some of her early performances and artwork have a prankster quality. For instance, she made "talking sculptures" by building speakers into musical instruments (she began violin lessons at age five). In the summers of '74 and '75, on the streets of New York, Anderson performed *Duets on Ice*, playing a violin altered to include a built-in speaker so that prerecorded music could be heard in conjunction with her live sound. She wore skates frozen into a block of ice, and in keeping with performance art's focus on real time and duration, the show was over when the ice melted.

Throughout the seventies Anderson's indoor solo performances mixed words and visual images, combining poetry, stories, dreams, songs and projections. In 1980 her recording *O Superman* became the number two song on the British pop charts. With this success in the music business, Anderson became arguably the best-known performance artist.

In both her recorded music and live performances, Anderson's intelligent sense of humor and strong personal presence are apparent. In the recent *Empty Places*, she cut a powerful swath across the vast Brooklyn Academy of Music stage in her spiky hair and man-cut suits, making her violin wail. As in the earlier *United States*, Anderson explored the ways in which communication between people is affected by technological interference and social neglect. In deceptively simple, ironic lyrics, she comments on our attempts, both social and individual, to gain control, and on the frequent backfiring and invisible costs of these efforts. In *Empty Places* it is Anderson herself who, in a hurry to get somewhere, steps from a cab into an open manhole. Lying injured at the bottom, she thinks, "This is exactly like one of my songs."

Anderson likes her work and life to be totally entwined. Being a woman informs her work now "more than in the past. When I started taking singing lessons I found a new voice—I'm really a soprano. I began writing differently—more from a female point of view." She thinks that seduction is "absolutely" a part of performing, for both men and women. "You have to feel sympathy or rapport or revulsion to care about what someone is saying. I'm another human being. Care about me."

Laurie Anderson's seven-hour, four-part United States *premiered at the Brooklyn Academy of Music in 1983. Parts of the work were presented as* Americans on the Move *at the Carnegie Recital Hall and The Kitchen in 1979. The complete text of* United States *was published by Harper and Row in 1984. Excerpts from Anderson's work have appeared in publications such as* October, The Drama Review *and* Performing Arts Journal. *Songs from her most recent performance,* Empty Places, *are available on the 1989 album* Strange Angels.

from UNITED STATES

THEMES FOR THE PICTURES

I had this dream . . . and in it my mother is sitting there cutting out pictures of hamsters from magazines. In some of the pictures, the hamsters are pets, and in some of them, hamsters are just somewhere in the background. And she's got a whole pile of these cedar chips—you know the kind: the kind from the bottoms of hamster cages—and she's gluing them together into frames for the pictures. She glues them together, and frames the pictures, and hangs them up over the fireplace—that's more or less her method. And suddenly I realize that this is just her way of telling me that I should become a structuralist filmmaker—which I had, you know, planned to do anyway . . .

DOG SHOW

I dreamed I was a dog in a dog show.
And my father came to the dog show.
And he said: That's a really good dog.
I like that dog.

And then all my friends came and I
was thinking:
No one has ever looked at me like this
for so long.
No one has ever stared at me like this
for so long
for such a long time
for so long.

DEMOCRATIC WAY

I dreamed that I was Jimmy Carter's lover, and I was somewhere, I guess in the White House . . . and there were lots of other women there, too . . .

and they were supposed to be his lovers too . . . but I never even saw Jimmy Carter . . . and none of the other women ever saw him either . . .

And there was this big discussion going on because Jimmy had decided to open up the presidential elections to the dead. That is, that anyone who had ever lived would have the opportunity to become President. He said he thought it would be more democratic that way.

The more choice you had

the more democratic it would be.

from NEW JERSEY TURNPIKE

I was living out in West Hollywood when the Hollywood Strangler was strangling women. He was strangling women all over town, but he was particularly strangling them in West Hollywood. Every night there was a panel discussion on TV about the strangler—speculations about his habits, his motives, his methods. One thing was clear about him: He only strangled women when they were alone, or with other women. The panel members would always end the show by saying, "Now, for all you women, listen, don't go outside without a man. Don't walk out to your car, don't even take out the garbage by yourself. Always go with a man." Then one of the eyewitnesses identified a policeman as one of the suspects. The next night, the chief of police was on the panel. He said, "Now, girls, whatever happens, do not stop for a police officer. Stay in your car. If a police officer tries to stop you, do not stop. Keep driving and under no circumstances should you get out of your car." For a few weeks, half the traffic in L.A. was doing twice the speed limit.

NEW YORK SOCIAL LIFE

Well I was lying in bed one morning, trying to think of a good reason to get up, and the phone rang and it was Geri and she said: Hey, hi! How are you? What's going on? How's your work?

   Oh fine. You know, just waking up but it's fine, it's going okay, how's yours?
Oh a lot of work, you know, I mean, I'm trying to make some money too. Listen, I gotta get back to it, I just thought I'd call to see how you are . . .

And I said: Yeah, we should really get together next week. You know, have lunch, and talk. And she says: Yeah, uh, I'll be in touch. Okay?

Okay.

Uh, listen, take care.

Okay. Take it easy.

Bye bye.

Bye now. And I get up, and the phone rings and it's a man from Cleveland and he says: Hey, hi! How are you? Listen, I'm doing a performance series and I'd like you to do something in it. Uh, you know, you could make a little money. I mean, I don't know how I *feel* about your work, you know, it's not really my style, it's kind of trite, but listen, it's *just* my opinion, don't take it personally. So listen, I'll be in town next week. I gotta go now, but I'll give you a call, and we'll have lunch, and we can discuss a few things.

And I hang up and it rings again and I don't answer it and I go out for a walk and I drop in at the gallery and they say: Hey, hi. How are you?

Oh fine. You know.

How's your work going?

Okay. I mean . . .

You know, it's not like it was in the sixties. I mean, those were the days, there's just no money around now, you know, survive, produce, stick it out, it's a jungle out there, just gotta keep working.

And the phone rings and she says: Oh excuse me, will you? Hey, hi! How are you? Uh-huh. How's your work? *Good*. Well, listen, stick it out, I mean, it's not the sixties, you know, listen, I gotta go now, but, uh, lunch would be great. Fine, next week? Yeah. Very busy now, but next week would be fine, okay? Bye bye.

Bye now.

And I go over to Magoo's, for a bite, and I see Frank and I go over to his table and I say:

Hey Frank. Hi, how are you? How's your work? Yeah, mine's okay too. Listen, I'm broke you know, but, uh, working . . . . Listen, I gotta go now, uh, we should *really* get together, you know. Why don't you drop by sometime? Yeah, that would be great. Okay. Take care.

Take it easy.

I'll see you.

I'll call you.

Bye now.

Bye bye.

And I go to a party and everyone's sitting around wearing these party hats and it's really awkward and no one can think of anything to say. So we all move around—fast—and it's: Hi! How are you? Where've you been? Nice to see you. Listen, I'm sorry I missed your thing last week, but we should really get together, you know, maybe next week. I'll call you. I'll see you.

Bye bye.

And I go home and the phone rings and it's Alan and he says: You know, I'm gonna have a show on, uh, cable TV and it's gonna be about loneliness, you know, people in the city who for whatever sociological, psychological, philosophical reasons just can't seem to communicate, you know, The Gap, The Gap, uh, it'll be a talk show and people'll phone in but we will say at the beginning of each program: Uh, listen, don't call in with your *personal* problems because we don't want to hear them.

And I'm going to sleep and it rings again and it's Mary and she says: Hey, Laurie, how are you? Listen, uh, I just called to say hi . . . . Uh, yeah, well don't worry. Uh, listen, just keep working. I gotta go now. I know it's late but we should really get together next week maybe and have lunch and talk and . . . . Listen, Laurie, uh, if you want to talk before then, uh, I'll leave my answering machine on . . . and just give me a ring . . . anytime.

FALSE DOCUMENTS

I went to a palm reader and the odd thing about the reading was that everything she told me was totally wrong. She said I loved airplanes, that I had been born in Seattle, that my mother's name was Hilary. But she seemed so sure of the information that I began to feel like I'd been walking around with these false documents permanently tattooed to my hands. It was very noisy in the parlor and members of her family kept running in and out. They were speaking a high, clicking kind of language that sounded a lot like Arabic. Books and magazines in Arabic were strewn all over the floor. It suddenly occurred to me that maybe there was a translation problem—that maybe she was reading my hand from right to left instead of left to right.

Thinking of mirrors, I gave her my other hand. Then she put her other hand out and we sat there for several minutes in what I assumed was some kind of participatory ritual. Finally I realized that her hand was out because she was waiting for money.

RED HOT

My sister and I used to play this game called Red Hot.
And in Red Hot, the ceiling is suddenly about a
thousand degrees.
And there's no gravity.
Gravity doesn't exist anymore.
And you're trying not to float up to the ceiling
so you have to hold on to things.
You have to hold on to sheets, pillows, chairs,
anything so that you won't go floating up to that ceiling.
I guess it's not what anyone would call a very
competitive game.
You know what I mean?
Mainly, we just sweated a lot
and we were really glad when it was all over
and the ceiling cooled back down again.

THE
CONSTANT
STATE
OF
DESIRE

KAREN FINLEY

KAREN FINLEY

Karen Finley was born in Chicago in 1956. Her mother was a political activist who read Karl Jung and theosophy. Her father, a practicing Buddhist and jazz musician who read the Beat poets, Kerouac and Aldous Huxley, killed himself when she was twenty-one. The oldest of six children, Finley participated in the Chicago Art Institute's Young Artist Studio program from the time she was twelve. There she met performance artist Jim Grigsby, who introduced her to the concept of not having a product, of the importance of process. "The idea of not having an object seemed so radical politically to me."

Studying painting at the San Francisco Art Institute, Finley realized that "it was mostly Abstract Expressionist and it was mostly men. I really started feeling the absence of women in the art world." She also began noticing that "women had their power sexually rather than economically or politically, so I started talking about that in my work."

The performance artists who affected her most—Chris Burden and Vito Acconci, Gina Payne and the Kipper Kids—used their bodies in their artwork, a practice Finley carried on. While working with Harry Kipper (her husband then), Finley performed in nightclubs, circumventing the art gallery circuit. She wanted to "put emotion into performance, like expressionism into painting" and to make work "that people could understand, that would have references to the world rather than to the history of art." She found that her raw, highly charged pieces suited the energy of the club setting.

To create a work, Finley does research about a subject that interests her (for instance, behind *The Constant State of Desire* is Betty Friedan's *The Feminine Mystique*), then enters a state of deep concentration. Her work comes from "an emotional commitment to something I feel very urgently about and that needs to be changed now."

Finley is tall and lean, with long brown hair which she often piles on her head. She has a mobile, expressive face and characteristically closes her eyes when she shifts from a casual, seemingly improvised chat with the audience into the words of one of her characters, whose voice seems to come from deep within, as though some lost soul is speaking through her.

> The psychic world is very important to my family. I did go to psychics and I have worked as a psychic. I think that somehow works with Catholicism. When I was eight years old we would have times at school where we were supposed to put our head down on our table and imagine our guardian angel behind us. That's a very powerful idea, that you see the invisible.

The Constant State of Desire *premiered at The Kitchen in New York City, in December 1986. Karen Finley has performed it in San Francisco, Chicago, New Orleans, Boston, Washington, D.C., Milwaukee, Berlin, Helsinki and other American and European cities. This text was previously published in* The Drama Review *(Spring 1988). Finley's book* Shock Treatment *will be published by City Lights Books in the fall of 1990.*

THE CONSTANT STATE OF DESIRE

ACT ONE

Enter in yellow dress. Hair in chignon. Monologue from overstuffed chair.

BABY BIRD

She dreams. She dreams of strangling baby birds. Bluebirds, wrens, and robins. With her thumb she pushes back on their beak, against their soft small neck till it snaps like a breaking twig.

She dreams. She dreams of being locked in a cage and singing loudly and off key with her loved ones standing behind her whispering very loudly. "She has an ugly voice. Doesn't she? She has an ugly voice." Oh, leave it to the loved ones. To judge us like they do. It's always the loved ones who always interfere with our dreams.

She dreams. She dreams of falling out of a fifth-story window. But she catches her fall by holding on to the window ledge. It's January and the ledge is made of stone and icy cold. The stone, the ice, the cold cuts through her flesh, her fingers, her bone. It doesn't matter though, for she has ugly fingers. And she sees the blood gush out of her limbs, the harder she holds on to the ledge. She can hear her own death. And her husband walks below as she hangs out of the building. But her husband hadn't memorized her shadow and she didn't know how to wear perfume. She wasn't that kind of a girl. So she calls out for help. Help. Heelp. Heelllllp. But the wind was in a mean mood and took her cries halfway round the world to a child's crib, so its mother could hear her own child's cries.

This dream was considered very important to the doctors. For in the past she had dreams of tortures, rapes, and beatings where no sounds would come out of her mouth at all. She'd open up her mouth and move her lips but no sounds would come out at all.

But she knew that these doctors were wrong. For these were the same doctors who anesthetized her during the birth of her children. These were the same doctors that called her animal as she nursed. These were the same doctors that gave her episiotomies. No more sexual feelings for her during and after childbirth.

But she knew that it really wasn't the doctors' fault. That the problem really was in the way she projected her femininity. And if she wasn't passive, well she just didn't feel desirable. And if she wasn't desirable, she didn't feel female. And if she wasn't female, well, the whole world would cave in.

Like when Martin died. Like when Desi Arnez, Liberace, Danny Kaye died. What is happening to my heroes? They are all dying on me. And Desi will never get back with Lucy. All of my boys are dying on me. All of my babies are dying on me. Oh, I wish I could relieve you of your pain. I wish I could relieve you of your suffering.

Like when my father finally told me he loved me after forty years then went into the bathroom, locked the door, put up pictures of children from the Sears catalog, arranged mirrors, black stockings and garters to look at while he masturbated as he hung himself from the shower stall. Whatever turns you on, girl. It's that ultimate erection. It's that ultimate orgasm. Whatever turns you on. Whatever, whatever turns you on.

And when he died—volcanoes erupted, cyclones appeared, coyotes came out of their caves, old people were struck by lightning. Don't you know that I don't want any more deaths on my conscience?

For I already have an abortion on my conscience from when a member of my own family raped me. Don't worry, I won't mention your name. Don't worry, I won't mention your name. And the reason why my father committed suicide is that he no longer found me attractive.

And by now you can tell that I prefer talking about the fear of living as opposed to the fear of dying.

ACT TWO

Easter baskets and stuffed animals sit on table. Take off clothes. Put colored unboiled eggs from basket and animals in one large clear-plastic bag. Smash contents till contents are yellow. Put mixture on

body using soaked animals as applicators. Sprinkle glitter and con-
fetti on body and wrap self in paper garlands as boas.

Scene I

HATE YELLOW

I hate yellow. I hate yellow so much. And I see you walking down my neighborhood with your new teeth and solid pastel-colored shirts. Yuk. Don't you know that I'm only happy when I'm depressed? Don't you know I'm only happy when I'm wearing black? That I'm only happy at night. Yes, I'm a creature at night.

NOTHING HAPPENED

So I took too many sleeping pills and nothing happened.
So I put a gun to my head and nothing happened.
So I put my head in the oven and nothing happened.
So I fucked you all night long and nothing happened.
So I went on a diet and nothing happened.
So I became macrobiotic and nothing happened.
So I went to the Palladium, the Tunnel, and nothing happened.
So I went down to Soho and checked out the art scene and nothing happened.
So I quit drugs and nothing happened.
So I worked for ERA, voted for Jesse Jackson and nothing happened.
So I put out roach motels and nothing happened.

So I petitioned, rioted, terrorized, and organized and something is going to happen. Something is going to happen 'cause I'm not going to let you gang-rape me anymore walking down my streets that I built with my soul, my creativity, my spit. And you just look at all of my art, Mr. Yuppie, as just another investment, another deal. My sweat, my music, my fashion is just another money-making scheme for you. You are the reason, Mr. Entrepreneur, why David's Cookie McDonald's is the symbol of my culture.

You are the reason why fast food is the only growth industry of this country.

TIE YOU UP & STEAL YOUR BMW

So I take you Mr. Entrepreneur, Mr. Yuppie, Mr. Yesman and tie you up in all of your Adidas, your Calvin Klein, your Ralph Lauren, your Anne Klein too, your Macy's, your Bloomingdale's. I tie you up in all of your fashion, your pastel cotton shirts of mint green and lilac and you know what? You like it. You like it.

So I open up those designer jeans of yours. Open up your ass and stick up there sushi, nouvelle cuisine. I stick up your ass Cuisinarts, white wine, and racquetball, your cordless phone and Walkman up your ass. And you look up at me worried and ask "but where's the graffiti art" and I say "up your ass." And you smile 'cause you work all day and you want some of the artistic experience, the artistic lifestyle for yourself after work and on weekends.

So I take your yuppie body and let you lick the piss and shit off me on Avenue B. Just let your tongue lick the artistic experience, the attitude off of that street. Then I make you lick the tires of your BMW. Then I leave you on the street and I steal your BMW 'cause I know nothing is going to happen.

So I drive the BMW down the street at full speed. Scaring to death anyone who looks like they hold a political office, anyone who looks like they own private property (I'll show you the burden of private property), anyone who wears a suit. 'Cause you know according to Mr. Andy Somma suits and rock 'n' roll don't mix.

CUT OFF BALLS

I drive down to Wall Street and break into the Exchange. I go up to all the traders and cut off their balls. They don't bleed, only dollar signs come out. They don't miss their balls 'cause they're too busy fucking you with everything else they've got.

So I gather all their balls, scrotum, testicles and stick 'em in my mouth. I roll 'em around my mouth and I feel like a squirrel in heat. I love the sound of scrotum. I take the balls home and boil them. 'Cause they're small balls and need to be plumped up. After I boil the balls I roll them in my own dung, my manure. 'Cause I'm the Queen of the Dung Dynasty. The I roll the Dung eggs in melted Hershey's Kisses. Then I roll the scrotum, manure, chocolate-coated balls into fancy foiled papers from found Eurotrash cigarette boxes. Now I've got gourmet Easter egg candy to sell. I sell these Easter eggs to gourmet chocolate shops. And I love to see nine-year-old boys who only communicate with their computers eat their daddies' balls. I love to watch all of you Park Avenue, Madison Avenue know-it-alls eating your own chocolate-covered balls for twenty-five dollars a pound.

I get my revenge. Oh, I get my sweet revenge.

Lord, why don't you appear to me now?!

Is it because you're a man?

Whatever happened to the Tooth Fairy? Whatever happened to the Easter Bunny? Whatever happened to Andy Warhol?

Dead, girl. Dead.

I know I live in a dead-end time. A dead culture, a dead-end world. I know I've got a dead-end job. Got dead-end housing and a dead-end future for my kids. I know it's a long, long dead-end road. A long, long dead-end road.

Ruenne. Ruenne sleeps with a gun under her pillow. For every time she has intercourse with her husband he defecates uncontrollably as he has orgasm. And the shit is running loose and splatters. Even though she puts down Hefty trash bags over the carpeting and walls, lets the crap dry before pulling it off the plastic, she found the gun to do a better job. She puts that gun in her husband's asshole every time he is about to cum. The gun up his ass gives her such a sense of power. And for a few fleeting moments the tables are turned for her as she forgets the time when at gunpoint she was forced to perform fellatio in front of her children and pets in her own garage.

And Father when I said good-bye to you before I went off to war, you were too busy with your head in the toilet to reply. I just wanted that fatherly hug to a son turning to a man. No, you had to puke your gin, rye, and whiskey in the toilet bowl. And I never forgave you for that. And they sent me to Vietnam on Christmas Day to eat a meal of gray. To clean a dead man's gun, to sleep with an old wound for a blanket. And every man, child, and woman I killed was my father's face in that toilet. And I prayed I'd die at war so my father would learn guilt. I told myself it would be different when I had children. We'd share our experiences and feelings together. We'd be so close. But I'm just like my father, a drunken slob.

And the only feelings I share are no feelings at all. Just no feelings at all. The only feelings I share are no feelings at all.

Scene 2

Return to chair in same costume as Act One.

FREUD

It was really Freud's problem to begin with.

Really. You don't say.

Yes, rumor has it Freud had been sleeping with his daughter and sister-in-law on repeated numerous occasions.

I knew it. That beard and that book on cocaine.

What I wanted to bring up today though is that all fetuses are innately female for the first six weeks.

Is that so. Then that means that perhaps the penis and scrotum are merely an exaggerated clitoris and labia?

Perhaps.

Well, I hope you aren't going to tell me the theory that woman was man's first possession?

Oh, no. I wouldn't dream of saying that. I merely wanted to suggest that it wasn't love that motivated man but the need to possess and master!

Isn't that a little harsh?

The truth is harsh. What are you making for dinner tonight?

Richard's favorite, Hungarian Goulash.

Don't you enjoy women's studies' classes?

I certainly do. All of the books. All of the subjects. But if it ever got in the way of me being a proper hostess for Richard's business I'd give it up in a minute. I'd sacrifice anything for my family. To the point of being a boring and phobic person.

Is that why you get headaches?

I'm sick and tired of your asking me about my headaches, my ways, my life. Don't you know that my illness is all I have? That my headaches are my only form of nurturing? My disease is my life, my health. Sure, I take Valium. But how can I look at my daughters and sons and try to dispel the myths that have been a tradition for centuries? To just say, "Sure, we're all created equal." I've never been treated equally my entire life. That

I'm supposed to be excited that Mary Boone Gallery signed up two women. Wow. Yeah, big fucking deal. Like I'm supposed to be *so* thankful 'cause a chick is on the Supreme Court. You can read your fucking books. But nothing's changed. Nothing has changed.

So let me continue. The one thing then that man could not destroy was woman's ability to produce children that loved her unquestioningly. And even though the man was stronger than the woman slave he could not destroy the bond between the mother and her children. And the father learned that he must earn his child's love.

So maybe it's womb envy instead of penis envy?

Perhaps.

This must've made the father very jealous indeed. Especially when he discovered the woman's ability to produce multiple orgasms. Okay. I know some of you guys think you can fuck a couple of times in a row. Big fucking deal. We never have to wait to refuel. Just keep on going.

Perhaps that is a way of looking at it.

So actually man put woman into a position of passivity when it is really the woman who is sexually superior.

Perhaps. But don't ever let them know it!

PARANOIA

LET ME TELL YOU ABOUT PARANOIA. Sixty percent of the world's commercial fish stocks are in danger.

Let me tell you about obsession. Grown men force-feeding young boys to produce the perfect shit. The perfect-size shit. The perfect-smell shit. The perfect-color, -size shit. In the toilet he slowly drops the turd out of his big pink butt. Let it drop, drop, drop and suck the turd up. Let it drop. Then suck it up!

Let me tell you about POWER. Being gang-raped by a group of youths at the age of fifteen in the subway. Until they discover my secret of being born without a vagina. They throw me onto the train tracks with their embarrassment and the train rolls over me. And all my mother could say was "See, the reason why God didn't give you a vagina is so that you wouldn't be violated in this way." So I knew I couldn't be a mother or whore so the only occupation left was religion. Until I discovered that God is a man. So I spend my life thinking of a time when virgins had babies and miracles happened to the meek.

And we all discussed our psychological disorders. Gary had overdosed, fell into a coma, and imagined tigers and angels dancing on his neck. Rachel imagined she had cancer and all of her organs were infected. Rita washed her hands all night long till her hands were chapped raw and bleeding. Jeffrey heard voices. One told him to marry Manson. Two told him to kidnap Mrs. Stern and impregnate her, and three to become Jody Foster's bicycle seat.

ACT THREE

FIRST SEXUAL EXPERIENCE, LAUNDROMAT

My first sexual experience was at the time of my birth, passing through the vaginal canal. That red pulsing tunnel, that alley of love. I'm nothing but a human penis. And at the time of my birth I had an erection. I'm fucking my own mama at my birth. It's the smell, it's the sight of my mama that keeps me going. Keeps me kicking.

So I spend my life looking for hot mamas with hot titties in hot laundromats. I go out in my real car. The symbol of my masculinity, cruising for mothers. I love to find a hot, young mama with a young, bald baby. A brunette, a pageboy. And she wears a pink gingham dress, the symbol of her martyrdom. I love the smell of the dryer, the sound of a spin cycle, the sight of a woman working a machine. Oh, it gets me going, seeing a woman's body against a vibrating machine. I just take that mama and push her against that washer. And I take her baby, a bald-headed baby, and put Downy fabric softener on baby's head. Then I strap that baby around my waist till it's a baby dildo. Then I take that baby, that dildo, and fuck its own mama. 'Cause I'm nothing but a motherfucker. I'm nothing but a motherfucker. Just puttin' that baby back where it belongs. Back to its old room, the womb. Back to its old room the womb. And then I take out those titties. Hope the bitch is still nursing. But she's a dried old cow, a dried old sow. A DRIED OLD SOW!!

AND THEN I BLACK OUT.

AND IT'S TWENTY YEARS LATER.

AND I'm in my mama's house.

And my mama is still watching the stories. The stories are still on. Oprah is on with a story on incest. *Dallas, Dynasty, The World Turns* too.

She's sprawled out on the avocado-green shag carpeting wearing her washed-out plaid housecoat. Safety pins pinned all together. I never knew why she wore all those pins. Like rubber bands round a door knob. Ooh, those pins excite me. 'Specially pins near sagging old flesh. And she smokes her Pall Malls, her Camels, her Pall Malls. Flick THAT ASH MAMA! FLICK THAT ASH! Look at me! Look at me! You never looked at me. No, you didn't. I'm nothing to you.

And there's tomato soup on the stove, macaroni and cheese on the fire, fish sticks in the oven. All that good white trash eats. Let me make your stick into a fish stick. The tartar sauce is free. No diaphragm cream needed here. So I'll roll my mama's belly onto the shag carpeting. She still not looking at me as I roll up her dress to the small of her back. She still not looking at me. She still watching that show on incest. And I look at her fat thighs and ass. Like uncooked bacon. My hands soothe her rumpled dimpled flesh. My mama! My mama, sweet mama. And I pull down her cotton Carters all pee stained. Elastic gone. Then I mount my own mama in the ass. That's right. I fuck my own mama in the ass. 'Cause I'd never fuck my own mama in her snatch. She's my mama.

I cum real quick. Cuz I'm a quick workingman. Work real fast. After I cum, I come outta my mama. She don't look at me. Just suckin' her Pall Mall. So I go down on my mama and suck my own cum outta my own mama's ass, outta her butthole. Her coconut Hershey juice. Suck it out. Suck it. Pucker. Pucker.

When I got my mouthful of the stuff, after I felch her good, I move my hands to my mama's face. I touch her red-and-white temples. Her potato face. I can see the raspberry lipstick leak into the wrinkles of her skin. That space between her lips and her nose. What's that space called? And I gently take the cigarette out of my mama's mouth. 'Cause if I got it wet she'd BEAT THE HELL OUTTA ME. She'd beat the hell out of me. I press my lips to my mother's mouth. And from the corner I spit back my cum into her mouth. Like pearls from an oyster into the sea at last. She just swallows the cum quickly, just keeps on staring at that incest show. Takes a drag out of Pall Mall and says, "Boy, you got lazy-ass cum. Your cum ain't salty. You can cum on my pancakes anytime."

REFRIGERATOR

And the first memory, memory I have, I have of my father, is he putting me into the refrigerator. He'd take off all of my clothes and put my five-year-old bare bottom onto the silver rack of the icebox. My feet and hands would get into the piccalilli, the catsup, the mustard and mayonnaise. My arms held on to my Barbie, Ken, Aunt Jemima, and G.I. Joe. All my dollies would protect me. All my prophets, princesses, and kings would stay with me. My Winnie-the-Pooh. You wonder why I throw up all of my food, whenever I see any condiments I gotta puke. Gotta upchuck all over the house.

Then my daddy is laughin'. Then my daddy is playing. Then my daddy gigglin' and smiling. Don't you know I hate smiles and laughter. Don't you know I hate good feelings! 'Cause the only feelings I show are NO feelings at all, girl. Just no feelings at all.

So my daddy plays behind the icebox door. Then he opens up the vegetable bin and takes out the carrots, the celery, the zucchini, and cucumbers. Then he starts working on my little hole. Starts working my little hole. "Showing me what it's like to be a mama," he says. "Showing me what it's like to be a woman. To be loved. That's a daddy's job," he tells me.

Next thing I know I'm in bed, crying. I got my dollies and animals with me. And I've got Band-Aids between their legs. They couldn't protect me but I'll protect them.

Then I hear my mama come home. And she starts yelling at the top of her lungs. "Whatever happened to tonight's dinner? Whatever happened to the vegetables for the dinner for tonight? You been playing with your food, girl? I wanted to make your daddy's favorite."

And I just cry to myself.

"Oh, mama open up those eyes. Don't you know that I'm daddy's favorite."

Is this what it's like to be a mama? Is this what it's like to be a daddy? No, this is what it is like to be part of the whole human race. And I'm your eldest son. I'm your middle, your youngest, your only son. I'm your son. Named after you. Your name.

When I told you that after all of my years of searching that I finally fell in love with another man. I fell in love with Louis, with Charles. You didn't believe me 'cause you never were in love before. Love didn't make the world go 'round for you. Prestige did. What others thought did.

I hadn't seen you for years. You had disowned me for my honesty of my sexual preference. You call yourself a doctor, a man of compassion. And when I told you I had the disease that mostly afflicts homosexuals, women, and children too, I know you no longer considered me your son, a man, so I went to you as a human being. And all you could say was, "I told you to stay away from those faggots, those fairies, those queers, those queens, those people with the lisps. I told you to get out of San Francisco."

Oh, Father, Father. You wonder why I send you a crate of shit each day. You call yourself a doctor who relieves pain. Man, you've been giving me nothing but pain since the day I was conceived. You call yourself a father, provider, the punisher, the moneyman. Baby, you sure been punishing me.

And when I died—you wouldn't even announce my death. Oh, no—you just called it accidental, cause unknown, uncertain. How could you announce my death when you never announced my life? Your fucking reputation. Your fucking reputation. Not even a proper burial. Not even a mourning for those who loved me. Oh Father, Father.

Call him the punisher, the provider, the moneyman.

I'm going to curse you Father till the day you die. Going to curse you from the grave. Blame you and God too. You might take my body away but you can't take my soul, my spirit, my mind.

It's the father in all of us that gives us the Berlin Wall, saves the whales, makes treaties, makes decisions and reasons, bridges and tunnels, cures diseases, ways and means. Politics and social disorders. It's the father, it's the father, it's the father in all of us.

And I pray to you Father in the sky every night. "Father, make me feel wanted. Oh, make me gain that unrequited love." Oh, it's the father. It's the father in all of us.

FIST FUCK

And after I fist-fucked you with my handful of sapphires, emeralds, garnets, and opals. Aquamarines, gold, silver, and platinum. I was fucking you with my will, my property, my esteem, and my values. I was fucking you with pearls and diamonds. Just filling your hole with everything I got. I was fucking you with my talent. That's all I got left. My rings just cutting you. And you just lie there bleeding. Your snatch on liquid fire. I just look down on you. You look up at me with your blue eyes and say, "It's better to feel abuse than to feel nothing at all. It's better to feel abuse than to feel nothing at all."

VOMIT BELLY

And I just collapsed on your pregnant belly and vomited, for I saw Mr. Reagan on the TV. There is a TV camera up his butthole looking up his asshole for polyps, for his colon cancer. He is so obsessed with what not to put up the butthole. So obsessed with what not to go up, up the ol' shithole. Had to sit with Rather/Jennings talk about yo' old polyps every day. Boy, I call your disease a metaphor. I call your disease your personal metaphor of being a fuckin' pain in the butt. I'm puking, man, on your liberty, your state of the union.

And I had to go out and get some air. I walked on the street and I saw you lying there on the sidewalk crusted in filth and neglect. I walked right over your baked body in the cement. My heel caught the needle in your arm, and tore your flesh with my walk. I knew you once. I knew you when you were to do great things for us. But now you are worthless. 'Cause I know it's every man for himself in this town, it's such a small city. Such a busy busy town. Just keep on walking, keep your head high. Just walk right over 'em.

ANKLES

And I just remembered the custom of our nation during war—of tying pregnant women's ankles while they are giving birth. Such a civilized culture. Such a great great land. Such kind peoples.

And after a few minutes there was quiet on the battlefield.

And we all exchanged names of our cats and dogs, memories and smells were evoked like our mothers used to show us when we weren't supposed to cry.

Let me tell you how I like brocades in woolen coats, the sweet scent of magnolia on your breath, the soft spot behind your ears. Let me tell you how I look at young men in blood-soaked costumes. Let me tell you how I look at young women undressing behind closed doors.

Let me tell you how I look at children dancing in their parents' blood.

I'm your voyeur. I'm your exhibitionist. I'm your pervert, your fool, your martyr and fool. I'm your Donald Trump, your Baby M. I'm your real estate, your profits, your greed.

But something's gotta give.

Something's gotta give.

Something's gonna happen.

M Y
BRAZIL

RACHEL
ROSENTHAL

RACHEL ROSENTHAL

Rachel Rosenthal, the daughter of assimilated Russian Jews who were patrons of the arts, was born in Paris in 1926. "My father, a prominent businessman who imported precious stones and Oriental pearls, was known as the "King of Pearls," so of course I was a little princess. If ever there was a Jewish princess I was it." In Paris she lived a sheltered and privileged life, full of British governesses, ballet lessons, and concerts in her parents' salon by Heifitz, Horowitz and Menuhin.

This privileged existence was shattered by World War II and the Nazi rise to power. Rosenthal's family left Europe for Brazil when she was thirteen (providing the subject matter for her 1979 *My Brazil*), and shortly thereafter came to the United States. On the boat to New York in 1941, her father heard about the High School for Music and Art, which Rosenthal attended after a summer in Los Angeles, where she was "appalled" by the style of life: "The girls were into makeup and stars and boyfriends. It was so far from me and everything that I thought or experienced—a big shock." Back in New York at Music and Art, she studied painting and visual arts (Alan Kaprow was a classmate), and performed in theatre, although her father strongly discouraged this activity. "He had very nineteenth-century ideas on the subject, to the effect that all women in theatre were whores."

After graduation from high school, Rosenthal spent her twenties going back and forth between New York and Paris. "At the time Paris was the center of new theatre and New York was the center of new art. So I got the best of both possible worlds." In France, she read Antonin Artaud's *Theatre and Its Double,* which greatly influenced her. In New York, she became friends with John Cage and Merce Cunningham, Robert Rauschenberg and Jasper Johns.

I always used to envy people like Bob Rauschenberg, who knew who they were early on. I was so filled with complexes, so filled with self-doubts. For one thing, I had this idea that to be an artist you had to be a man. If I'm a woman I can't be an artist; if I'm an artist I can't be a woman.

In 1955, when Rosenthal was twenty-nine, her father died. "It was really after my father's death that I was truly able to become who I was. I was so identified with my father and had such adoration for him that I had avoided doing anything that smacked of theatre." After his death, "I came to California and created Instant Theatre, which was totally improvisational."

At the time I was very involved in Zen Buddhism, which I had picked up from John Cage. In Zen you get this sense of being a butterfly going through life from instant to instant. They had just coined the phrase "instant coffee" and I thought Instant Theatre was a fun play on words—both Zen and pop. I felt the moment of being was sacred, and that was what you lived for, and therefore there was no such thing as preparing for the future or building on anything.

Instant Theatre existed for ten years. In 1975, Rosenthal, whose theatrical skills were honed by years of working improvisationally, realized that "the kind of work being called performance art was work that I had done under a different name for years." She made a reentry into the art community by way of the women's movement.

Rosenthal, whose physical appearance is strong and powerful, is a commanding performer. In various personas, sometimes bordering on the grotesque, she combines autobiography and social criticism in visually stylish performances that often use slides, props and music. In *Rachel's Brain,* she first appears as a weird Marie Antoinette, wearing blue-black lipstick and a sponge wig with a frigate on top. When her parody of eighteenth-century rationalism is over, she is beheaded— signified by a swift removal of the wig to reveal her shaved head. Later, she wears combat fatigues and wields a knife as cauliflowers drop from the ceiling while a slide of the human brain is projected onto the back wall. While she talks about looking for the secret to the brain, Rosenthal chops the cauliflower into pieces.

As with other performance artists, the autobiographical emphasis in her work has become more global in the eighties. She is very aware of her audience, and tries to influence the way they think by transmitting her own passionate concerns about ecology and animal rights.

The wonderful thing about performing is you're really like a high-wire artist. You have to be self-centered almost to the point of being obnoxious, otherwise you don't have the stage presence that you need. I absorb the power of the audience when I come onstage. It's a very physical thing . . . I take it in like a big vacuum cleaner. Then you give the power back to the audience by loving it. No matter how strong and mean and nasty the content of the performance may be, the actual doing of it is a gift of love.

Rachel Rosenthal's My Brazil *premiered at I.D.E.A. in Santa Monica, California in 1979. The drummer was Anthony Canty. Rosenthal learned all the Brazilian songs during the Carnaval of 1941. Her performance texts have been published in several journals, including* Performing Arts Journal *and* High Performance, *and in the book* Scenarios. *Her* Gaia Mon Amour *was published by Hallwalls.*

MY BRAZIL

A Recital

A 4' × 8' platform against the wall. Sheets of Mylar hang from ceiling to floor and line the sides of the platform. There is a stool stage left on the platform and a microphone on a stand stage right. Two sparklers and a lighter are placed on the platform, upstage.

The lighting is in pink, lavender, green, blue-green and blue tones.

A PA system with two large speakers. An audiotape runs through the speakers.

Before the performance, an assistant distributes both sparklers and matchbooks to the audience. The matchbooks are silver, with "My Brazil" by Rachel Rosenthal etched in green on the covers. The assistant tells the audience to light up when Rosenthal does.

Blackout. A male voice on tape.

The New York Times, July 16, 1940. "Readers of this newspaper have been able to learn from Mr. Russel B. Porter's informative dispatches in recent weeks what the Nazi menace is like in Brazil. In Mr. Porter's opinion it already amounts to an *undeclared war*. The Nazi efforts are deliberate and unmistakable. Spying, terrorism, economic pressure, physical violence, the boycott, misuse of the schools, the radio, newspapers, the motion pictures—all have been used and each is used as circumstances permit. The tricks are precisely those employed by the Nazis in the Balkans, in Scandinavia, in Holland, Belgium, Spain and France. If Hitler has not yet laid claim to the million Germans of Southern Brazil there is every sign that he will do so whenever he feels strong enough. The 'Dry War' has, in short, been brought to this hemisphere by the Nazis."

Segue into "O Que Que A Bahiana Tem," a vintage record by Carmen Miranda, sung in Portuguese. Record ends.

Lights. Rosenthal enters, accompanied by the Drummer. She is wearing a Grecian-type turquoise gown, high heels, and a white orchid in her hair. The Drummer is black, stripped to the waist, wearing white pants and Yoruba beads. He carries a large conga drum and is barefoot. They step up onto the platform.

Rosenthal and the Drummer bow to the audience and to each other. He sits on the stool and she picks up the mike from the stand. She sings a cappella:

JARDINHEIRA

Jardinheira porque estás tão triste?
O que foi que aconteceu?
Foi a camélia que caiu do galho,
deu dois suspiros e depois morreu.
Oh Jardinheira, O meu amor!
Não ficas triste nesse mundo,
é tudo seu e tu es muito
mais bonita que a camélia que morreu.

Rosenthal then steps downstage and the Drummer taps a simple beat. She talks and swings her hips.

Sometimes I prune a Creeping Charlie. I cut off the small piece and place it in a glass decanter with water. I pinch it first. It reacts as if goosed. Some weeks later, the decanter water turns a greenish hue. Vague clouds of green meander about aimlessly, gathering momentum. The Charlie forages with a newly harbored white Chinaman's whisker, says good-bye, and emigrates to dirt. The green scum sloshes angrily awhile and then subsides. I lose interest and pay attention elsewhere. It's all assumed to be as it is, as it was, as it always will be. Appalling, isn't it? I grow complacent. Will I die not having known the rapture of the deep? I can't swim too well in all this algae.

On muggy days I look up and see a timber wolf sitting quietly on my doorstep, watching me discreetly. When Mother was about to die, she saw the Wilis, in white tutu, like in *Giselle*. She was afraid of spooks. I'm not afraid of wolves. The decanter sits on the sill, filling with slugs and water moccasins. I dreamt it was a Trojan Fish, filled with piranhas. One day, I pick up my objects and find them all brittle and light. Desiccated and eviscerated. All empty pods. Whatever happened? Time sends me messages in envelopes but forgot to insert the note. Something is going to brush me gently with its wings, I'm sure. Never say die! I anoint myself, just in case. Don't laugh. When I stop suiciding, I'm a robust Queen of the Jungle. And I rarely need a straitjacket nowadays, which was difficult to tie anyway since I insisted on doing it all myself. But I suffer from Life's Cramp. I am dying.

The Drummer stops. Rosenthal sings:

AURORA

Si você fosse sincera
ô-ô-ô-ô Aurora
veja só que bom que era
ô-ô-ô-ô Aurora!
Um belo apartamento com porteiro e elevador
e ar refrigerado para os dias de calor
"Madame" antes do nome você teria agora
ô-ô-ô-ô Aurora!

The Drummer resumes, with a slightly more complex beat. Rosenthal speaks, and her dancing becomes more accentuated.

When I lived in Tarzana, just before the events that led to my leaving home, I was swimming in our pool one day, when I happened to look up at the sky. Way up there, very high and very small, was what I later recognized to be a white sheet of paper, waltzing and zigzagging in air currents, ascending, descending, dancing its gradual approach to earth. For some reason, I couldn't take my eyes off it, and it became a kite, with my gaze the string it was attached to. And I reeled it in, slowly but surely, until that piece of paper fluttered down into the pool beside me, within two feet of where I was standing! I felt singled out somehow, and vaguely heard a call, but didn't recognize the voice.

A long time ago, a similar event took place.

I was with my parents, high above Rio de Janeiro, at the base of the forty-foot Christ on top of Corcovado mountain. It was in 1940. Some new friends took us sightseeing in their car. It was just before the rainy season and the sky was stridently clear. As I was walking around the big statue, I was eyeing uneasily a huge, jet black butterfly flapping about in the hot, still air. I had a butterfly phobia. Suddenly, a gust of wind swept him away in the direction of the sea. I looked out at the string of sparkling bays in the white-hot sun under the cycloramic blue sky. And then I saw a black cloud, like a tiny spot on the horizon. The air around us began to churn. The black butterfly was whirled back as I watched that speck of black cloud racing toward us at vertiginous speed, progressively blotting out the blue of sky, until it was all around us, the wind howling, huge raindrops pelting us as we ran for the car and as the black butterfly fought for balance trying to reach the shelter of the jungle growth. We raced down the mountain road, but by the time we reached bottom there was an ocher-colored flood in the streets and our car fairly floated.

I know today but didn't know it then, that I had died as I am dying now. I was also born then, in Brazil, in 1940. This corpse was born in Rio, age thirteen, the product of a cosmic upheaval and a very private alchemy.

The Drummer stops. Rosenthal sings:

HELENA

Eu ontem cheguei em casa, Helena,
te procurei mais não encontrei.
Fiquei tristonho a chorar . . .
Passei o resto da noite a chamar.
Helena, Helena, vem me consolar!
Depois de cansado
teu nome eu chamava baixinho.
Helena dos meus encantos
Vem me fazer um carinho.
Eu fiquei desesperado,
cadê Helena meu bem?

O dia ja vem raiando e
minha Helena não vem.
Porquê será?

The beat is now lilting. Rosenthal is dancing the samba during the next text.

There is an awesome theory of quantum physics called the Many Worlds Theory. It states that all possibilities in the wave function of an observed system actualize, but in different worlds that coexist with ours. Who is in these worlds? We are. In other words, the choices between various possibilities are illusion. With each and every choice we make, the world splits into separate and mutually inaccessible branches, each of which contains different editions of the same actors performing different acts at the same time, on different stages that are somehow located in the same place.

In 1940, there is a Rachel who sailed across the Atlantic. There is another Rachel who remained in France. The Rachel who stayed splits into a heroine who fought the Germans in the Resistance, and another who hid like a coward in some remote countryside with secret cellars filled with hams and sausages hanging from the rafters. Either Rachel or both split again, into one who survives and one who is caught by the Nazis and tortured. That one divides into she who tells all, causing the deaths of many, and she who dies in a concentration camp, having allowed the abject desecration of her body in order to save her soul. The Rachels who survive become, one, a "grande bourgeoise" married to a snob, two, an artist, whose modernist tastes are shaken in 1948 with the arrival in Paris of John Cage and Merce Cunningham, whom she meets, befriends, and follows to New York. But wait a minute . . . . That wave function must have joined with another and merged, for I was there, in Paris, in 1948, and I met Merce and John . . .

Anyway, the other wave function that brought me to that point crossed the equator on the Atlantic in September 1940. The others, all the others, in their equal and separate universes, are somehow and inexplicably a part of me as well, as I am of each and every one of them. I am the hatred of the Germans, the fear of the knock in the night, the coward, the horder, I am the hero parachuted behind enemy lines, the horror and nausea of torture, the panic of incarceration, the guilty survival and the battered death.

The Drummer stops. Rosenthal sings:

ALA-LA-O

Alá-la-ô ô-ô-ô ô-ô-ô!
Mais que calor ô-ô-ô ô-ô-ô!
Viemos do Egito
e muitas vezes nós tivemos que rezar:
Alá! Alá! Alá, meu bom Alá!
Mande agua pra Ioyô!
Mande agua pra Iayá!
Alá, meu bom Alá!

A strong, rolling beat.

Before I was thirteen, I dreamt recurringly of being swallowed by a tidal wave, relaxing into it, and experiencing bliss. The wave appeared over the horizon like those gigantic Picasso "Women at the Beach" of his surrealist period. In Rio, 1940–41, I played in the Copacabana surf. The waves were often twenty feet high and higher. My girlfriend Janine and I would let ourselves be sucked into the huge wave's undertow, maneuvering and calculating so that, at the exact moment when the wave was about to break into bone-crushing white water, we would propel ourselves with superhuman effort out of the accelerating suction and dive into the glaucous green underbelly, emerging on the other side, battered and breathless, ready to face the gathering of power of another colossal wave. It was fantastic! I didn't fight the waves. I tuned my body to resonate with equal power. I heard the mighty rhythms and obeyed them. To fight would have broken the flow, and the wave would have shattered me to pieces on the sand.

In the sea, I was a hero. Out of the water, I was a tadpole: large head, my body trailing behind me like a snail-trail of mucus. I had abandoned in the Northern Hemisphere the blood clots of first menstruation and the muddy bogs of pubescent feelings. I was in love with my brother Pierre. In Brazil, I spent hours on my bed, eyes closed, drowning in nostalgia and making Proustian efforts to recapture the feel, the smell, the exact taste of love and lust lost. At night, macumba drums wafted from the many jungle-covered little sugarloaf hills of the city, I slept in a hammock, a lion of lights glided across Botafogo Bay advertising Lyons Tea. "When the war is over, Pierrot!" I would whisper like Scarlett O'Hara to Ashley. Pierre was killed in North Africa, a great hero and posthumous Croix de Guerre and Legion d'Honneur, in the Sahara Campaign of 1943.

I am experiencing death in a very real way. In my body. There is an entropic tendency below the skin. I dream of devilish geometries in an attempt to organize this sloppy information. I dream that Satan slices a man in four with his eyes, each quarter neatly encased in skin, like grapefruit segments. They fall to the floor, shaped like a swastika. I also dream of letting my animals die, untended, in some forgotten room.

In Rio, a business acquaintance of my father's, a man called Pereira, sought to ingratiate himself to us by bringing me baby animals that his men caught in the jungle. The first was a baby anteater. I called him Tatú for that was his name in Portuguese. The Tatú slept in my bed, I didn't know how to feed it or what to do. I was always afraid he'd escape and fall down the elevator shaft. Later on, Pereira brought me a baby alligator. We put it in the bathtub. He created even greater problems. We were invited to the *fazenda* of Monsieur and Madame Hammond, for Christmas. The Hammonds owned a small zoo and we decided to bring them the animals. We placed them in boxes, with breathing holes. The *fazenda* was in Terezopolis, in the mountains above Rio de Janeiro. We took a little wooden train that cranked us up the steep mountainside, surrounded on both sides with virgin forest. The jungle was impenetrable, emerald green, overgrown with pink and white orchids, and teeming with brilliantly colored birds. All the way up, the little train stopped in villages where the cars were besieged by dozens of vendors, women in multicolored skirts and turbans carrying piles of fruit on their heads, little boys with baskets of *guaraná* (the Brazilian Coke), men with trays of pastries covered with flies, everyone laughing, shouting, singing . . . . For the duration of the trip, the Tatú panicked. He kept pushing his little snout desperately through the breathing hole and struggling. I could see his little eyes filling with pus. When we got to the *fazenda*, he was ice-cold. He died within a few days. The last time I saw the alligator, he was in a bathtub, again, only this time with a frog that someone had placed there. The two were eyeing each other mournfully.

The drumming stops. Rosenthal sings:

EU NESSE PASSO VOU ATE HONOLULU

Eu nesse passo vou até Honolulu, ô-ô-ô,
ô-ô-ô-ô, devagar!
Lá no meu clube só se dança o kanguru ô-ô-ô
das dêz as três sem parar.
Parece valsa, fox-trot, tango, rumba,
hula-hula e macumba,
até maracatu, uh!
Pois lá no clube toda gente cai na dança
leva no colo criança
pensa até que é kanguru!

A fast, samba beat.

I feel I am in the process of being sucked into a black hole. At what stage does one stop fighting it? There must be a point in time and space when all is in balance, poised, where all stands still, and then there is a tremendous, cosmic sigh, and one gives in, and all becomes easy, the pull of the hole accelerating toward the singularity, where being and annihilation coincide, where you are squeezed for an infinitesimally tiny moment into the singular essence of what you are, and then you emerge on the other side, unrecognizable even to yourself, but with the roaring pulse of matter burst forth from the womb! I can't wait . . . . Not because I'm in such a hurry for all this, but because the oscillating tension between being a hero or an asshole is killing me!

The drumming stops. Rosenthal sings:

O-O-O OPA! QUE DANCA SOPA!

O-ô-ô Opá! Que Dança sopa!
que os Indios sem roupa
me ensinaram a dançar.
Todo mundo diz que vai, mas não vai
e fica pulando no mesmo lugar . . .
O-ô-ô Opá! Que Dança sopa . . .

A very sensual rhythm. Rosenthal has been dancing more strenuously to the various rhythms as she speaks. The movement is dissociated from the words and spoken rhythms.

Brazil! Site of the second chakra! Sexual susurration of the language — a Portuguese caressed and tongued into insinuation and quasi-obscene nakedness. The colors of sex: red, orange, gold, green, purple . . . . The dance. The dance everywhere. The imperative of the dance. Its demands, its orders. The abandon of all non-Dionysiac modes. The singleness of purpose of the life-force, buttressed by anxiety, lonesomeness, fear. The billows of love. I am tunneled with love as by maggots. I am rotting with love. Nowhere to cast it but back on myself and my father and mother. Watertight. Self-enthralled. I am an infant again, cradled and rocked, but this time in my mother's arms. I am the center of the world. I am enervated. I have leapt feet first into dependence. I wear a dogtag. I am a slave of love. My thirteen-year-old infant flesh imbibes it. My head inflates with fear. I am encephalitic for a week. My head is so swollen and painful that I can't move it from side to side on the pillow without screaming. The doctors can't diagnose.

And how could they? Other refugees complain of sores between their fingers, of toenails turning soft and falling off. Tropical diseases, we say. The truth is that our bodies are liquefying under the impact of a world where fortunes are squandered in three bacchanalian days, where gorgeous black bodies always ripple to audible or silent beats, where forests are studded with myriad orchids like millefleur tapestries gone wild, where giant cockroaches fly, and where there are two dozen different kinds of bananas. Brazil is there for the taking. My father is poised, with grandiose plans. We are ready, Daddy Vampire, Mommy Vampire and Baby Vampire, to bite into the succulent land. But we didn't. Jews are jailed right and left. Some even disappear. One day, the American consul calls, "off the record," and tells Mr. Rosenthal to heed his brotherly advice and be on the next boat to the U.S. within four days.

And we were. Abandoning the diamond mines and real-estate bonanzas to the Fifth Column. We had lived in Brazil seven months. During that time I died, I was born, I was weaned, reimprinted and bonded for good. I may even have been dwarfed and bonsaied too. I don't know if I ever grew up. Worse yet, I don't know if I'm a giant compared to the Rachel who stayed.

The drumming stops. Rosenthal sings:

E NO BOLIMBOLAIXO

É no bolimbolaixo
que eu quero ver você!
É no bolimbolaixo
que eu quero ver você!
Bolimbolaixo
bola em cima
bola em baixo!

A slow beat.

I am falling. My arms and legs, flailing the ether, become swastika-shaped. I spin faster and faster. This stigma at my core must melt. When I learned of Pierre's death, my face screwed up into a grin. Negation. Refusal. Amputation and death. I cannot love, except the beasts. I atone for the Tatú. Pierre had the sharp muzzle and luminous eyes of a wolf. I spin and spin and the branches of the swastika melt away, flowing in an unbroken circle. I must liquefy this accursed sign that saws me into a duality no longer liveable and that robs me of the last, the only wave.

Vision: a Nazi rally. Huge stadium. Floodlights. People in thirties clothes. A hundred thousand heiling soldiers. I swoop down on them, tear their backs open with knives, hoist them up with meat hooks, decapitate them with swords. Then I am with Pierre, at the Borj des Monopoles, in Tunisia, where he is alone, having ordered his men to fall back, manning a machine gun, facing the advancing Germans. We are together, machine-gunning hundreds, in intoxicating syncopation. He is hit in the chest and the head. All around us, in the Borj and along the flanks of the adjoining cliffs, are bodies of German soldiers, bleeding. Countless rivulets of blood trickle down to form a lake of blood. From the depth of the lake, black dinosaurs surface. They are like huge bubbles and they float up into the air. Pierre grows. He grows taller than the hills. Taller than the clouds. Then he flays himself and his skin falls off like a banana peel. His form remains like a pillar of light. He picks me up in his arms and together we fly over the Earth. The beautiful, the dazzling Earth. We glide over meadows covered with flowers. Over oceans and mountains. Over Grand Canyon. We then leave the Earth and fly to the

Moon. And from the Moon to each planet of the system in turn, including Jupiter and its moons, Saturn and its rings. We leave the system and fly to the stars, the nebulae, the distant galaxies. Pierre becomes a cosmic cloud and tells me: "I am everything. I will teach you from all there is." I leave him and return to Earth.

The drumming stops. Rosenthal sings:

"COWBOY" DO AMOR

Quando monto o meu cavalo e jogo laço
prendo logo, prendo logo um coração.
Sou Cowboy mas gosto muito de um abraço:
"Mãos ao alto! e não vai dizer que não!"
Sou vaqueiro capataz de uma fazenda.
Nas horas vagas também toco o violão.
O meu cavalo
está ensinado a
tomar bilhete para a filha do patrão!

A very strong, rolling beat. Vigorous dancing.

Yes, I am searching for the perfect wave, knowing full well where it's been all this time. When I was little, I had trouble skipping rope because I couldn't jump into the circling rhythm. One day, I will close my eyes and take a flying leap. Then, I and the flow will stand still, in perfect unison, watching the river banks speed by. I will cuddle up inside the wave's curl forever, the roar of the water in my ears, silence in my heart. Then slowly, but with progressively lovelier configurations, I will break into splashes of drops like fireworks, waterworks, sparks. I will shatter and re-form in an infinite variety of ways, landing on my feet, my fins, my claws, my beaks, my trunks, my antennae . . . . I will fly with the fish and dive with the birds. I will be a geyser and a waterfall. I will be a black water spout and a white tornado. I will erupt from Krakatoa and evaporate in Mono Lake. I will perspire from your pores and drink myself from a straw. I will have fulfilled all the promises and be none the wiser. I will become what I have always been and go back to where I never left. So if one day you cannot find me, just remember: I will be Missing In Action!

TEENY
TOWN

LAURIE CARLOS
JESSICA HAGEDORN
ROBBIE MCCAULEY

LAURIE CARLOS,
JESSICA HAGEDORN,
ROBBIE McCAULEY

Collaborating under the name "Thought Music," writer/performers Laurie Carlos, Jessica Hagedorn and Robbie McCauley teamed up for *Teenytown,* a work staged from their individual writings. The connection between these women is deep, based on their shared personal concerns and common interests in music and poetry. "Our work works together, and we have a kind of music between us. Thought music." Each of the women has a daughter, which seems important to their collective and individual explorations of traditions and connections.

An indictment of individual and global racism, *Teenytown* retained the autobiographical emphasis of the seventies and extended it into the larger social arena. In it, the combination of these three voices—Laurie's is lyrical and imagistic; Jessica's is biting and sarcastic; Robbie's is direct and enraged—is both disturbing and exhilarating.

Robbie McCauley was born in 1942 in Norfolk, Virginia but spent most of her childhood in Georgia and Washington, D.C. She came to New York in the mid-sixties and got involved in experimental and black theatre, working at La Mama, Caffe Cino, the Negro Ensemble Company and the Public Theater. "What I wanted to do was to be, as an actor, a part of the creative process. I didn't have any name for it at that time but I loved working close to audiences, having the work of creating the play." She also went to the New Lafayette Theatre, where "jazz theatre" was being developed—a loose form where the actor's voice provided a rhythm for the dialogue. She met Laurie Carlos in an acting class taught by Lloyd

Richards at the Negro Ensemble Company, and became close friends with her when they played together on Broadway in Ntozake Shange's *For Colored Girls Who Have Considered Suicide/When the Rainbow Is Enuf.*

While working Off-Off Broadway as an actor, Robbie supported herself as a social worker. "It was a job, but it was also part of the sensibility I was starting to develop and hone. I wanted to take in personal experiences that are the result of social conditions and be able to speak on them and I thought theatre could do that." Her work is "based in the South in the storytelling, in the experience of being brought up in what I now easily call apartheid because it was that—the signs were there when I was a kid." She often uses personal family history in her work, addressing the absence of blacks in written American history by telling the stories of her ancestors. Her first solo work was *My Father and the Wars,* in 1985. "Since then I've been shaping other works out of that concept of the personal and the historical." She is currently developing *Sally's Rape,* using her great-grandmother's children by the white plantation master as a metaphor for a larger pattern of rape and domination of blacks by whites in this country.

Jessica Hagedorn, who is a poet, novelist and playwright, was born in Manila in 1949 and moved to California as an adolescent. After studying theatre at San Francisco's American Conservatory Theatre, she concentrated on writing poetry and short fiction and helped edit a literary anthology published by a Third World artists' group.

In the early seventies she met kindred spirits Ntozake Shange and Thulani Davis. "All three of us were interested in doing poetry in collaboration with artists working in other media."

> I had never given up the idea of performing. I was really drawn to music. I thought that poetry was a tradition that was very musical. So I formed this band, the Gangster Choir. I didn't know about performance art, I just called it a poet's band. A band where the musicians would not just play music. They might be called upon to do some text, do some acting. We would break up songs and do fragments of things I was writing. It was a form that had no rules.

By 1978 "the scene was winding down," and after a number of visits to New York (during one she met Laurie Carlos) Jessica made the move east, leaving the band behind. In 1981 Hagedorn's *Tenement Lover*, directed by Davis and incorporating a smaller version of the Gangster Choir, was staged at The Kitchen. It addressed "themes that continue to obsess me—otherness, the idea of revolution . . . dominant culture vs. so-called minority culture. And the idea of home, what homesickness and home mean." Laurie Carlos became a coperformer and writer in the New York band.

Laurie Carlos was born in Manhattan in 1949 and raised on the Lower East Side in a family of eleven children. Her father was a drummer and her mother a dancer. "There were always a lot of people in our living room, harmonizing, doing their steps."

As an actor, Carlos "had a real affinity for writers. I've always been interested in making writers' visions come, in finding dramatic lines and making stuff work." She worked with a number of poet/playwrights, most notably with Ntozake Shange. By 1981 she'd left *Colored Girls* and was writing a piece called *Someday the Dialogues Will Begin Themselves* with Thulani Davis, who had introduced her to Jessica Hagedorn. "I wanted to take that work and some other work and put it all together and create some kind of performance piece that addressed loneliness, mostly." The piece was finally called *Shadow and Veil*. She asked Robbie to be in it, asked Jessica to direct, put her nine-year-old daughter Amber in it, and got a space on 125th Street from Roger Furman to do the show. "The vision I came to *Colored Girls* with I finally actualized with Jessica and Robbie and my kid, in Harlem, with Roger Furman."

For Carlos, *Colored Girls* was about self-definition. "The women we were didn't exist in the theatre. We were going to finally define for ourselves, through our bodies and our voices, exactly who we were in the world." Both in their individual projects and in their work together, the women in Thought Music continue to follow this aim. Their initial collaboration was a real turning point for them. As Laurie remembers it,

> We were beginning to find our own voices. There were no venues for what it was we wanted to do. None. None in any black world, in an Asian world, there were none in a white world. Performance art was the one place where there were so few definitions. The way that we have conversations, what occurs across time zones, what memory is, what color is, how music affects movement and memory and the

texture of breath has nothing whatsoever to do with the Eurocentric playwriting form. The dust comes through the window, the rat cries in the corner, and . . . you start screaming. That's what we're living with. So that is what we're trying to do in our work.

In *Teenytown*, Thought Music uses a minstrel-show format as a political statement, and also because this episodic variety structure lends itself to making a performance from the individual texts by the three writers, and the two they wrote together. "What we call minstrel shows were based in the black tradition in a positive way. We did a lot of research into how the history of this form relates to racism." The first half of the piece uses traditional style; the second half uses the television talk show as the model for the modern minstrel show. The writer/performers wanted to explore racism in popular culture through a form that is accessible and provocative.

A collaboration of writer/performers Laurie Carlos, Jessica Hagedorn and Robbie McCauley, and visual designer John Woo, Teenytown *featured choreography by Jawole Zollar. It premiered at New York's Franklin Furnace in February 1988 and was performed at the Danspace Project, St. Mark's Church, in June 1988.* Teenytown *includes three traditional minstrel characters: Jones (Hagedorn), Bones (McCauley) and the Interlocutor (Carlos). In the Danspace production, two additional performers, Sam Jackson and Ching Valdes/Aran, also took on these names.*

Jessica Hagedorn's publications include two volumes of poetry, Dangerous Music *and* Pet Food & Tropical Apparitions *(both Momo's Press), the play* Tenement Lover *(in the anthology* Between Worlds, *TCG, 1990) and the novel* Dogeaters *(Pantheon, 1990). Robbie McCauley's writing has been published in* Catalyst, The Portable Lower East Side *and* The Poetry Project Newsletter. *Laurie Carlos's pieces include* Nonsectarian Conversations with the Dead, Organdy Falsetto *and an expanded* White Chocolate.

TEENYTOWN

THE PROLOGUE: MINSTREL MANIA

Offstage, the three writer/performers are heard singing "I don't know, but I've been told, / If you keep on dancing, you never grow old."

They come out one at a time, take on exaggerated show biz and minstrel gestures, and freeze. They sit in three chairs, play makeshift instruments (washboard, miniature ukelele and accordion, spoons, cooking pots) and sing "Swanee River," "Dixie" and "Bandanna Babies." They freeze in minstrel pose.

An elegantly dressed couple, guest performers, enter. They dance a diagonal tango to a Cab Calloway song. The man drags the woman offstage.

The trio jump up and do a series of racist, sexist jokes.

Carlos sings "Summertime."

Hagedorn and McCauley, as Dorothy Dandridge and Hazel Scott, two glamorous black entertainers from the past, perform "Razz-matazz" by Carlos; Carlos, as a sort of Oprah Winfrey character, reacts to them in a segment called "The Interviewer," written by McCauley. Dorothy Dandridge is dressed in a polka-dot flamenco dress. Hazel Scott wears an evening gown.

Razzmatazz	The Interviewer
DD: My husbands had to be white. I was too sexy.	
	I am bewildered by some of the stuff that surfaces.

HS: My husband had to look white. I was too outspoken. I played the piano. I liked to dance.

I am shocked by the incidents that occur.

DD: Hollywood is too hard without a white man. The world's a bitch without a Jack not a Joe. A Joe, good or not, would never do. There is still no cure for a nigger gone bad with kisses.

I am astounded by the incidents that happen.

HS: Kisses from a rich dark woman gave them no time to think. My husband had to look white I played piano I listened to my mother.

I am knocked down by the things that come up.

DD: I wanted drugs with no association to singers, they let me overdub I had good legs I had a recipe for good head. You need that in Hollywood when you can't stop crying when you can't even sing the blues.

I am overcome by the passions that emerge.

HS: Remember only the good not the bad. Not the burnt eggs not the death threats. I had good legs. They respect my hands. I loved Paris like the song.

I am bewildered by some of the
stuff that surfaces.

DD: The sheriff's deputies that
carried me away were all
white one was Joe and he
had not washed that day. I
love greens, and Hattie was a
real lady. I want my Joe. Is
there still the blues?

Carlos sings "Summertime" again as Dandridge and Scott fade out.
Carlos and Hagedorn take the poses of back-up singers. McCauley
becomes a torch singer and performs her piece "Pork" a cappella.
The back-up singers repeat "pork" and do steps and gestures as
comments on their role.

PORK

I once lost a friend from eating pork.
Everybody was hungry, it was a late-nite munch,
it was a soul-food restaurant, real commercial,
but conscious enough back then to ask if you wanted
beef or pork ribs.

We'd shared stories of old aunts and
other roots down South. Neither of us
had ever been dirt poor, she was younger,
had gotten further away, I was uncomfortable
with something about her ease in America.

When I said "pork" to the waiter, her eyes
went up outta sight. With serious Black bourgeoisie
nationalists back then, you didn't eat pork. I
wanted to say "I'm sorry, it was a slip of the tongue,
a bad habit, I'll change my order." But I didn't.
I wasn't ready to tear down the walls that had grown
up mortared between us . . .

I remember I was opening doors inside myself.
I remember that the sauce on the ribs was awful,
mainly ketchup, and there was no more conversation.

It was years before I gave up red meat altogether
for health reasons and years later that I was able
to say, "I am a Black *revolutionary* nationalist/in-
ternationalist, that the struggle is a protracted one,
we are all in it, and that many of the contradictions
are resol—va—ble."

*The male performer enters with a mop which he turns into a micro-
phone and a machine gun. He comes out as "the janitor" and trans-
forms into a series of characters—rap artist, black militant, preacher—
as he performs McCauley's "Assassination Improvisation."*

ASSASSINATION IMPROVISATION

Thinking about the assassin in me
just fantasizing which is
something we all have a right to/it's
really just an image
being artiste-ty. thinking about
the assassination. where it could be.
in a meeting for the international
something or other you could go
flip bang shut the door
just a thought just an image thinking
about the assassin in me,
I mean, they think up the darndest things
why can't we? I'm thinking about the
assassin in me, can think what I want to
can't I? Thinking about the assassin in me . . .

*When he exits, Hagedorn, Carlos and McCauley each perform a
piece—"Hail Mary," "Monkey Dance" and "Georgia Mud" respec-
tively—which relates to where she comes from. While the trio tell their*

stories, the elegant female character, her mouth taped, moves slowly across the upper balcony, doing angular gestures.

HAIL MARY

1956 1957 1959
Cora Aguilar
so tough
swiveling her hips
just so—
the right snarl
on her pouty lips

Cora cuts her long black hair
into a perfect Polynesian pompadour
lacquered with cheap pomade,
her dazzling rooster's crown.

she is the "female Elvis of the Philippines"
more man than Eddie
more Elvis than Elvis
swollen & immortalized
on his bed of plastic roses.

divine pulp
& corny love
the nasty drawl
& innuendo
of your delicious poetry
Otis

she masters phonetically
and spits out with passion
swaggering behind
her suggestive guitar

Cora
all brown and muscular blaze
sinuous onstage—
a natural.
her guitar was the real thing,

electric—

Otis.

1956 1957 1959

MONKEY DANCE

I go camping outside on the drive looking for Canarsie. "They got a fishin' place there."

   My clothes are stuffed under the bed! I'm ready like a fleet of rubber ducks in red beak. The world is a shiny place in this downtown where all who were coming came to get theirs. The river defines status! "Give it one more try. If you say that's where the fish are then look for it." The air is not the same and there was gravel. More things to ponder over. Lips poked all the way out. Nothing looks like me or the way I feel. Everybody has a plan. My Keds are removable. I can't keep wearing these blouses without bleach. With my hair knotty, full of barrettes and rubber bands from Orchard Street. My stepmother found out about my father's girl-friend up the street, so we are not going to Brooklyn this year. She can't send us noplace Donna plays with herself and I tell everybody what I think about them. All these people got different names. I'm going fishing in Canarsie if I have to dream it again.

GEORGIA MUD

Feel like   sand in my feet
Feel like   brick pillar porch
Feel like   rain coming down
Feel like   sunshine
Feel like   feet in the mud
make a sandcastle house

Fee-eel like chinaberry tree skirt
switch around my hip
switch down the dirt sidewalk
switching down the street

Old ladies sitting on the front porch
rocking/say "Hey chile,

when you go—and we know
you gon' be the one what go, chile—
tell 'em what we know down here, chile!"

I am as old now as those old women were back then.

Feel like sand in my feet   sandcastle house
brick pillar porch feel like pine
feel like Georgia in the summertime
feel like pain   feel like red clay
feel like mud   feel like rain   fee-eel
like blood.

The trio perform "All Shook Up," by Hagedorn.

ALL SHOOK UP

did you know?   oh-oh
did you know
there are no   oh-oh
no no bananas
in France?   uh-oh!
Josephine's skirt *was* imported

c'est soir, les noires
uno, dos, tres
isa, dalawa, tatlo
ang tatay mong kalbo!
BON SOIR!

no good bananas in France?
absolutely. no, none.

did you know   uh-oh!
Otis Redding's new album
is not available

death is death
recordings are forever . . . uh-oh!

1. *(Robbie)*

"the king" is dead
but the real deal
has never been forgotten.

pulp songs stupefy some,
awaken others.
revolution's sentimental,
after all.

2. *(Jessica)*

confessions of an exotic exile:
"the definitive tango definitely took place
in Paris . . . years ago, strange fun at the Hotel Intrigue . . .
Little Algeria, the Latin Quarter—baby, couscous balungus,
every night!"

considered avant-garde,
the lovers partied hard . . . much too ahead
of their time.
they caressed & cajoled
their quivering prey:
"menage a trois is so French,
doncha think?"

those were the days! love me tender,
fierce celebrations of the Western Empire's
decline. that fuckin' curse worked every time—
"you plundered the planet, darlin'!"

VIVA LAS VEGAS! Elvis puffs up.
love decays so sweetly.

confessions of an exotic exile:
"apres le bain, en la grande cama de la
pequeño hotel room, the homely young musician
spreads her beautiful thick legs with reluctance.
a working-class Parisian, she is an experiment;
by the way, I never listen to Elvis."

a working-class Parisian,

she is an experiment: the exotic exile's
first and only white woman. such thighs!
the panting lovers sigh:
"you taste like the moon! you smell like
new-mown hay!"
or a cow, shy & moony—
the exile thinks, bending to kiss
her other lover.

3. *(Laurie)*

"the king" is dead
but the plagues
are now upon us.

build a fort
make soup
set fires
only pack what you can carry!

we're all shook up.

Paris is a stinking racist town
Argentinians refuse to serve
us steaks we don't even want—
WE WANT CAFE! CAFE OLE! THAT'S
ALL WE WANT YOU NEO-NAZI EXPATRIATES!

arbitrary & arrogant
gendarmes demand
i.d.
in crowded subway stations

we whip out passports
trembling with rage.
we dream of singing
right up in their faces
but we know better.
you know the rap—
"je suis une ugly americain, bébé!"
hiss that secret litany,
protection against evil spirits:

little richard,
fats domino,
chuck berry
otis uno
otis dos
otis tres,
fontella bass.

we're international citizens,
you understand.

"well/bless my soul/what's wrong wit' me/my hand is shakin'/and
my knees are weak/my tongue gets tired/when I try to speak/I'm
in love/I'm all shook up . . ."

Otis Blackwell
too
somewhere in Brooklyn
(better call him up)
he always said
you were smart

who wrote the song?
who gets the credit?
what's in a name
but the world—Elvis

"el vis" so pseudo French
so possibly Spanish—the sound of it bastardized,
redneck tender and cruel.
no big deal in a racist world

Otis Blackwell
always said
you were a smart girl
(better call him up.)

another otis,
sugar.
otis,
some name
otis

Elvis' famous flame
of black r & b mythology.

who wrote the song
who gets the credit

i tell you
that was many years ago
Paris still a racist town
but the subways are licked clean
by Algerians & Viet Cong
glass cases along tiled walls
displaying leftovers from the Louvre.

Manila's racist too—
don't let them tell you different.
it's always "mestizo" this
or "Amerikano" that—
the anxious watch for dark skin
and aboriginal noses.

is an old rule,
some say.
"you got to be hungry
to hip hop."
you got to be hungry
to rock 'n' roll.
everything else
pales by comparison.

Elvis—
the same rules apply.

what do we do?
too many rotten Spaniards
in the stew—
the Elvis Presley of the Philippines
a half-breed pretty boy
1959 1963 1965
now passé
Eddie Mesa is alive & well
in Brooklyn

where art is art
in spite.

*At the end, taking the poses of a church choir, the trio break into
"Blessed Tammy," a song by Carlos.*

BLESSED TAMMY

Oh Tammy Bakker
WE know God loves you
We know God loves you
Oh Tammy tammy

Oh
Tammy Bakker
We know God loves you
Because he told us
Told us to tell you

Oh
Tammy tammy
Oh
Tammy Bakker
We know God loves you
Told us to tell you
Oh Tammy
tammy oh tammy tammy oh tammy tammy oh

*Commenting on nontraditional casting, the three do random lines
from Shakespeare in ethnic accents as they get into place to do
"Teenytown" by Hagedorn. Seated, they do hand gestures and stag-
ger the lines among themselves; on certain words, they speak together; at other times, they alternate.*

TEENYTOWN

Once, there was a teeny tiny town ruled by a teeny tiny mayor . . . . Teeny
tiny goats roamed abandoned buildings and teeny tiny parking lots
strewn with rubble and teeny tiny garbage . . . . Everyone was always

hungry; you could see it in their tiny anxious faces and their teeny tiny eyes. (INCLUDING THE MAYOR!)

Teeny tiny boys and teeny tiny girls lived in teeny tiny mousetraps and ate cheese . . . . Five days a week, some of the more ambitious ones went to teeny tiny offices, smoked teeny tiny cigarettes, and slaved at part-time jobs where they never got to use their tiny minds . . . . No small matter. Two days a week, all the other teeny tiny boys and teeny tiny girls dreamed teeny tiny dreams which they diligently recorded on teeny tiny scraps of paper. A SLIGHT RIPPLE ON THE DIM HORIZON . . . A FAINT EXPLOSION FROM A DISTANCE . . . BUT A SHIT-STIRRER, NEVERTHELESS. To squelch rumors and prevent exotic and desirable aliens from ruining the neighborhood, the wily, teeny tiny mayor called town meetings on a monthly basis. Everyone was encouraged to complain at the same time, and when the noise died down, everyone always went away feeling much better.

At teeny tiny parties where no one was invited, teeny tiny poets compared dreams. They were always amazed at similarities in length and content; of course, it had been the same old teeny tiny town ever since anyone could remember—and they liked their dreams that way . . . . When the party was over (when the party was over), the teeny tiny poets fed their scraps to the ravenous, rabid goats who bleated, barked, and wailed in the squalid alleys outside holes they called "windows."

Days and nights passed in dissonant, familiar harmony—teeny tiny sunless days that turned without warning into terrifying moonless nights that seemed to go on forever . . . . The teeny tiny townsfolk took small comfort in promising each other that teeny tiny terrors could always be kept at bay. You know how the song goes: "You can be in my dream, if I can be in yours . . . "

In an homage to Stepin Fetchit, the trio performs the cartoon "dance shuffle," which comments on the footage of racist cartoons from the forties and fifties playing on the monitors.

Then all three do "Stinky Riff," by McCauley.

STINKY RIFF

Obsessed   w/smell
Better not smell bad!

go up on a high contralto
simile of disgust/turn your
nose up real *hiiigh*
if something stinks

ooooooooo . . . . *ooo!*   smell like
beat-up onions!
say the word nasty like it's
onomatopoetic—naaaasty!

Sister wd say stink w/the
country short 'a' over & over
percussive-like 5/4 time
STANK! STANK! STANK! STANK! STANK!
then extend it, adding the clarinet hum—
hu-um ummm ummmm umm!
then the lyrical coda, what it
was all about . . . . Girl! Don't you
go outta here smelling like no slave ship!

They repeat minstrel gestures as lights come down. Intermission.
    The silhouette of a man and a woman is seen behind the curtain as slides of racist and sexist stereotypes mixed in with historical images—lynchings, marches, police with dogs—are projected. As if doing a radio play behind a scrim, the man and woman recite the lines of "Dog Eat Dog," written by Carlos, Hagedorn and McCauley.

DOG EAT DOG

Male Voice:
Dog eat dog the world   doggone underfoot   underwheel   taxis dog
for dog doggone taxi down the runway dog it   doggone brownie the
tall black man in the brown suit had the decency not to cry on
Broadway on Broadway   not the Broadway of the Drifters   a Broadway
of spectacular cakes and beaded baby ballgowns underfoot underwheel

Hot dog the avenue of organza and pearl teardrops   the avenue of satin
he had the decency to keep the dog to keep the dog from being squished
to keep the dog he dragged it on the *Daily News*   on the Broadway of IRS
and crack deals on the Broadway of gaping mouths I hailed the taxi

He hit the dog going downtown I hailed the taxi going downtown
he hit the big dog again going downtown   doggone
god   the dog   was big

Voice #2:
I left the Philippines believing I would not need my recipe for dog-pie
   mush
I left knowing my taste for cognac would grow
don't step in the doo doo!

There's a fire raging behind you as we chat
and the telephone rings . . . I don't say a word
voyeur to catastrophe
you keep moving your lips in the silence

She's frantic with worry
"Don't step in the doo doo, children!"
She warns us before hanging up the phone.

There's a fire raging behind you
right there outside the window
a TV screen   your eyes smolder in flames

I left the Philippines with a recipe for dog barbecue
and my secret sauce
the delicious smell of singed flesh
on a Sunday afternoon

Savage like her memories of running dogs
and old men's humiliations

I moved uptown to know my people
and suck out the eyes of the dog dreams dog dreams
that chewed me raw
man's best friend and a woman's demise
we learn to suck bones   and stay cheerful

French poodle scuttles . . . . Rover retrievers . . . . Guard dogs & Schnau-
   zers with long ears . . . . Contest for running . . . and sitting . . . and
   barking . . . . Loss of identities . . . . Useless tags and falling hair . . .

Mange

CARLOS, HAGEDORN, McCAULEY

THE TONIGHT SHOW

Brash "theme" music accompanies the entrance of the three per-
formers, all in male drag—McCauley as Ed, Carlos as Doc, Hage-
dorn as Johnny. White dinner jackets over black tuxedo pants,
wingtip shoes: Johnny's jacket is covered with outsize buttons and
chains, Doc's jacket is pinned with 100 one-dollar bills, Ed's jacket is
silkscreened with paisley designs. The "guys" bow and shuffle, preen
and guffaw to canned laughter and applause, then go into their
opening "routine."

Instead of commercials, vintage racist cartoons and film footage
are shown on monitors at intervals throughout the show.

Ed: What did you do this weekend?
Johnny: Nothing. I stayed home.
Doc: Me too. It was great.
Johnny (*To Ed*): Just you and the kids.
Ed: That's right. It was great.
Johnny (*To Doc*): Say—where'd you get *that* outfit?

Ed and Doc bend over. Johnny, sharing "joke" with the audience,
kicks them in the ass.

Johnny: KNOCK KNOCK.
Ed and Doc: Who's there?
Johnny: Emmy.
Ed and Doc: Emmy WHO?
Johnny: Emmygrant!

The three performers laugh at their own jokes. In silence, they take
turns with classic "comedian" gestures. This happens in rapid suc-
cession, no more than three times.

Ed: Someone once told me. If Indians are Native Americans—then what
does that make me?
Johnny and Doc: Immigrant!

The three "guys" laugh and clap along with the audience. They exit.

The pair of guest performers come out as Bones and Jones and do a series of racist jokes. They exit and Hagedorn returns. The famous routine, the opening monologue, Johnny drops that playful golf stance.

Johnny: Very nice, Professor. Very nice. Your hairdo hurts my eyes. Whew! What a hairdo, huh? I don't know about image these days . . . do you? I mean . . . the semiotics can be very confusing. (*To anyone in the "studio" audience*) Hey man—you look like a car. How was your weekend? Yeah. I'm talking to you. (*Reacts*) Oh, nice. That's *nice.* Anyone here from Iowa? (*Pause*) I did nothing this weekend. Absolutely nothing. It was one of those weekends—you know what I mean? I woke up . . . crying. Couldn't remember my dreams, but woke up . . . crying. (*Shrugs*) Can you imagine—waking up, tears flowing from your eyes, your nose running, and a sob in your throat? (*Pause for punchline*) WHO DIED? I sat around the apartment all day in a daze. It was some kinda dread, folks. Some kinda terror. You know what I mean, right? (*Pause*) I was too depressed to kill myself. (*Pause*) You know the trouble with us is we aren't even niggers. I mean, what are we selling, and who wants to hear or see it? They already got niggers to entertain them. (*Pause*) Everybody knew I wanted to shout like Jackie Wilson, croon like Smokey Robinson, bend minds like Jimi Hendrix, outdance the Temps. Remember? They just thought I danced well. Filipinos can dance, sing, mimic any Hollywood movie. We hunger to be stars, desperately trying to please . . . . We're so damn exploitable, smiling, always smiling . . . . We'll probably smile our way into a revolution one day . . . shit. Too many fried bananas in our diet, I guess. I want to show you—I need to show you—that the other side to this madness is my mother's shy and frightened face when she gets on a bus. "EXCUSE ME, ex-cuse me," she whispers, apologizing for her life to everyone before she dares to sit down. And I listen to my father talk in his halting, broken English, look at his worn-out hands, the cracked skin like a map of the universe . . . *I am alien even to them.* They're permanent immigrants in this lousy place, and I've finally stopped asking myself why they never went home. (*Pause*) You know what I mean, right? We've all thought about killing ourselves at least once . . . . Yeah, yeah. I'm talking about you. There you are, nineteen years old, in a fire-engine red see-through negligee, choking on aspirins . . . . Maybe YOU'RE not white, but the world looks good and you got the answers, your tits aren't too big, your skin is luminous, and you're painfully aware you've got talent! What a burden. (*Pause*) Even your major disappointments are turned into artistic material. Every little second of anguish has value. *You're expressing yourself.* Spitting on the white male patriarchal Eurocentric gods and decolonizing your mind with gratifying drugs, shit shit shit and more shit piled on top of shit . . . bleak rock 'n' roll songs followed by part-time jobs . . . jobs stretched into more meaningful months than you've bargained for and all of a sudden your identity's in question! Are you an artist or a criminal or a whore or just an ordinary survivor? (*Pause*) HEY! LET'S DANCE!

Laugh track. Applause signs. Commercial break. Before Johnny exits, he again adopts that fabulous, playful golf stance.
McCauley comes out in her tuxedo, assumes a series of ballerina poses and does her piece "Sharks."

SHARKS

I *am* the darkskinned grandmother
have always been.

In the 6th grade the white
people chose six of us to dance
ballet on TV.

Poor darkskinned Miss White.
She had to tell me I couldn't go
because even though I was good
I was too dark & didn't have good hair
& they wanted to show the best on TV.

I never blamed darkskinned Miss White.
I never blamed the lightskinned girls they picked.
I never blamed the boy round my way
who told me to make sure to grease my legs.
And I sure didn't blame Mother and 'em
who always dismissed my expectations.

I understood. I've always been
the darkskinned grandmother.

& now they tell the dark daughters
we're beautiful. So what? Somebody's
beauty is a diversion. Where is the
Black *power*? They didn't co-op that
to sell fish grease with.

What's the matter with white people?
Are they so obsessed w/trying to be
sexy enough for something or other
that they can't even hear their own history?
I like white people who look history in the face.
Who admit they are thieves. From there, like they say
in group therapy, we can work.

> If the world has seen
> America through the
> movies, how do you think
> the world has seen me?
> I'm tired of explaining
> how it feels.

There is a place in the mid-Atlantic
where the sharks still go, after all
these years. They still remember the blood,
where millions of us got pushed overboard
midpassage, to rip us apart from ourselves.
They make sure our culture is forgotten.

My rage is enormous & I can hardly contain it.

A great liberal at the university
told how when he was in India
he saw two poor children
who loved each other
and he was amazed.

Well, in New York
I saw two ugly white people
in love w/each other
& I wasn't amazed at all.

I laugh to stop the rage

to stop the pain   had to
study to love myself   to see
my beauty. I can laugh so many
ways   behind my eyes   down my throat
chucking my chest   rocking my knees.

I carry my pain & sorrow
my rage & laughter like
a torch. I am the
darkskinned grandmother
& have been all my life.

> The man and woman do a contemporary, especially brutal Apache
> dance as they speak the text to "Sex and Death," written by Carlos,
> Hagedorn and McCauley. The man drags the woman off.

SEX AND DEATH

Death #1:
Sex again no mention of food, this time
sex again no mention of money or disease
he offers me a two-week vacation outside New York
outside television in a place of my choice

Death #2:
Sex again not even sex black-eyed peas & gladiolas
how real her savage memories collusion of cultures
sex again equals power equals manifest dancing anywhere
you wanna go

Dorothy rips open her blouse and bends over for the third time
BEND OVER I LOVE YOU stepping on a dime

Sex again how long can you give and you give and you give
tractors parked in lovers' lane heads thrown back
in discourse a foreign exchange a domestic truce per pound
no mention of food this time
va va voom
va va voom
va va voom

Dog dreams chew me raw
Africa rumbles in response
and she's
not even hungry

Carlos and McCauley come out and perform "White Chocolate/She and Her" by Carlos. McCauley, who plays She, the mother, wears a Lana Turner gold taffeta dress with high heels. Carlos is Her, the daughter, and wears a waitress outfit covered with fried eggs.

WHITE CHOCOLATE

Her: So there would be no Sunrise Semester. No Marty & Millie cartoons. You never knew who was on the couch or why. Who was this one asleep in the living room. Who was this in his shorts like he thought he was my daddy. From here he was short with a big ring on his finger.
She: Oh yes! That's a fabulous ring . . .
Her: That must be why she brought him home. Was he going to take us to Sweden?
She: Live for your dreams. Stand on the strength of your own convictions. When you . . .
Her: When she became a dancer she and Vernon Profit's mother were both making plans to go away. Vernon's mother I was told was going to Paris. So she would go to Sweden. People would ask when we were going? And if she had one like this we were going soon. When she worked in the pencil factory I could always get in the living room to watch the TV. Since she became a dancer and now a singer too, we had to stay in bed until the poets, songwriters, dancers and barmaids got off the couch, the floor, the big rose chair. Then in one of her voices she'd call us out to meet them.
She: His name is Otis. He writes songs. He writes music for the radio. He writes hits. He writes for . . .
Her: Then she said it. That name we hadn't mentioned since he said "all a nigger could do for him is tie his shoes."
She: He's famous!
Her: He's ugly!

She made me go with him to buy the things for breakfast. Eggs, bread, even orange juice and bacon from Abbey's. We rode the elevator down.

He wore a suit. I said "yes" a lot and he knew! You had to give Abbey a note for bacon. He would take you to the back and give you the package there. In the back is where you would see the numbers from the place they had been before. And you knew he was being kind to you. Out loud. Otis asked for the bacon out loud in the front. Didn't he know anything? We got kosher salami with the store full of people. Lloyd Archibald crossed my path asking when we goin' to Sweden. S-H-I-T. Otis told me what he would do if I was his child. And for at least the fourth time I informed him that I was not. My father is the most handsome man in the world. And why she would want somebody like him with those pop eyes? "You are a smart girl."

She: You are a smart . . .

Her: He did not play the piano well, only a few changes like Joe Webb. But I had heard blind Calvin and his fingers moved all around. We talked anyway after all he owned all the elevators.

She: Billie Dawn, Eddy Jones, Laura Webb, Ricco! Teddy Vann, & Champ!

Her: All the stores on Avenue D sold special. Mirch sold special! Toys at special prices. Mr. Max made shoes and he made special ugly shoes. Donna needed shoes every other month. Five dollars every time. Mr. Max could make you the same ugly shoes. The bakery was owned by a couple who had been married a long time. And the Chinese sold everything Chinese. Chinese . . . food. Chinese . . . laundry. Chinese . . . apples. Chinese checkers. Chinatown. Chinese

She and Her sing "Ching Chow."

She: Fabulous!

Her: I stood in the laundry waiting to pick up the sheets. This new man who was taking us to Sweden . . .

She: Where I go my children go. If you love me my children . . .

Her: This one had to have all the sheets ironed. He ran a booking agency. As soon as the lady came out I sang her my song. It was a wonderful day I told her. I told her see John O'Conner that's a boy in my class, he's in the third grade too. He asked me at the monkey bars to marry him. To be a bride with him. His father was a teacher at our school P.S. 188. And John's father and his sister were Irish. His mother was Irish too but she was dead so John and his sister came to school with their daddy. We gonna marry and have Chinese children. See he said I am pink and you are brown that makes yellow Chinese! So I told the lady I went to the Chinese restaurant and I sat down where the Chinese food lady could see me. And I thought about our pretty house with a place for everything. She came out from behind the counter and asked me what I wanted where was my note? "I want to see your children. Your children." She got her husband and I shook his hand. "I want to see your children." The children lived in the back I showed him where they were. They are cute I told John just like kittens. The fourth grade John was sent to a private Catholic school. His father said he would never come to 188 again. We laughed in celebration that day, I was happy, I was singing.

There are Chinese apples. Chinese checkers. Chinese children!
She: We are the same as ever. We are here. This is where we came to be free. Learn the difference between domestic champagne and French. Good clothes are good even second hand. (*She sings*) Enay ma tov u na nachiem she vech ahiem gon yah haugh . . . . Me casa es su casa en la dia en la noche en toda. Won't let nobody turn me around turn me around . . .
Her: First she moved to Brooklyn and then to Zaire in 1971 she has not returned. She made both moves alone with her children. She has never been to Sweden. (*She sings the Ching Chow song*)
She: Fabulous, fabulous, brava, brava!

> They applaud one another.
> The entire cast performs "Buck and Wing," an original aboriginal tap dance, in silence.

THE
SURVIVOR
AND THE
TRANSLATOR

LEENY SACK

LEENY SACK

Leeny Sack was born in 1951 in Brooklyn, the daughter of concentration-camp survivors who met at Dachau at the end of World War II. Without having experienced the Holocaust firsthand, she nonetheless felt an immediate relationship to it, "a woundedness from that experience, a sense of the family's wartime voice constantly mediating my own experience."

In developing *The Survivor and the Translator,* Sack "started with what I've always done, which is to start through the body. I was working with space, I was naked with a blanket, I had no words. It was so . . . dark. I had no anchors at all. It was too open. From there I went to the typewriter and the physical form I worked with then was sitting at the typewriter on a chair. That was enough of a container. It was a safe container. And I needed a tremendous amount of safety because it was such dangerous material."

Sack's approach was psychophysical and with language. Her own kinetic and linguistic explorations had grown primarily out of her work as a member of The Performance Group, directed by Richard Schechner; her studies in Kinetic Awareness with Elaine Summers; and workshops with members of Grotowski's Polish Laboratory Theatre. After a year of work, both alone and with trusted associates Steven Borst, Sabrina Hamilton and Chloe Wing, Sack began inviting friends to rehearsals of *The Survivor and the Translator,* gradually expanding the intimacy of her process. Several months after that she began public performances.

The intense physicality Sack used for the work challenged her physical endurance and heightened the spectator's sense of the urgency of the event. A vitality both emotional and visceral was transmitted. In the physical effort involved in performing the work, one glimpsed the emotional effort that went into making it.

The structure of the work reflected Sack's personal relationship to the material. The first part was "distracted and fragmented and 'this is how it made me crazy,' and the second part was coming to the point of simply being able to tell the story."

"The piece is very much about language and the way the failure of language is sometimes more articulate than precise and proper language. That mostly happens in the translation of my grandmother's testimony where she experiences constant circular failures of memory. Numbers can't really describe when it was or how long it was. She can't remember the word for "crematorium." She calls it "machines for burning people."

Making and performing *The Survivor and the Translator* allowed Sack to move on to another view of the world. She has an ongoing interest in awareness work, evident in her teaching, directing and performances. *Our Lady of the Hidden Agenda,* a performance about stigmata, originated from her interest in physical manifestations of psychic states. Her group work includes a project called *Paper Floor* that examines the relationships of movement, preconscious imagery and the physical act of writing. She lives and works at Pangea Farm, a center for the study and practice of contemplative and performing arts which she cofounded with psychotherapist and meditation teacher Norman Rosenberg in upstate New York.

The Survivor and the Translator *premiered in 1980 at the Performing Garage in New York City. Leeny Sack then took the piece on a six-month European tour; cities she performed in include Amsterdam, Paris, London, Cardiff, Milan, Florence, Antwerp, Brussels and Jerusalem. For her work Sack received a* Villager *Outstanding Solo Performance award and a Most Memorable Show award from London's* Time Out *magazine.*

The testimony in the text is from translated conversations with Rachela Rachman, the author's maternal grandmother. Also included is material based on, or from, The Last of the Just, *by André Schwartz-Bart;* The Kabir Book, *versions by Robert Bly;* Anne Frank: Diary of a Young Girl, *by Anne Frank.*

With thanks to Norman Rosenberg, Steven Borst, Sabrina Hamilton, Laura Rosenberg, Chlöe Wing, Rachela Rachman, Joel Sack, Alexander and Sonia Alland, Jr., for being part of this "solo" work.

THE SURVIVOR AND THE TRANSLATOR

**A solo theatre work about
not having experienced the Holocaust,
by a daughter of concentration camp survivors.**

To

Gina
1923–1989

**Gdzie moja mama? Nie widzę mojej mamy.
Gdzie, gdzie moja mama?**
Where is my mother? I don't see my mother.
Where, where is my mother?

Before each performance I place these things: an old white iron-frame bed; a backless and seatless rocking chair, also old and white; a white Sabbath candle in a tarnished silver candlestick; a book of matches. The bed must stand at an angle twenty-five feet from the first row of seats, the rocking chair seven feet from the first row. But they must be connected. I hang a long white cotton string between them, across the distance, one end tied to the bed, the other to the rocker. I make up the bed in its fitted black-and-white-striped sheet and center at the head the small airline pillow in its white pillowcase. I drape the white taffeta dress with the broken zipper over the foot of the bed. The candle in the candlestick and the book of matches go on the floor nearby. Centered on the wall behind the bed hangs a large white screen. On the floor between the rocker and the first row of seats stands a very old film projector.

On my head I wear an oversized set of black headphones with a long black coil-cord, long enough to stretch the whole length of the space. The end of the coil-cord plugs into a battered leather suitcase, is actually taped on to the side of the suitcase with torn pieces of black tape. I wear a white shirt and black pants and I am barefoot.

As the spectators enter I sit on the battered leather suitcase near the foot of the bed and whisper just audibly parts of the text I am afraid I have forgotten. But I have never forgotten. The story I tell was slipped under my skin before I could say yes or no or Mama. I sit inside the memory of where I was not. Yes. So there's no choice. That's what was.

When everyone is seated and settled I stand, face the wall to my right and proclaim in a loud flat voice, waiting for the echo at the end of each word:

LET
EVERY
WOMAN
INCLUDING
YOUNG
GIRLS
ADD
HER
HOLY
LIGHT
TO
ILLUMINATE
THE
WORLD
SHROUDED
IN
DARKNESS
AND
CONFUSION

I face the spectators and lower the headphones down around my neck. I speak as I walk toward the spectators, stretching the coil-cord from the suitcase across the length of the space to where I stop. I stop center, three feet from the first row of spectators, and speak directly to them:

> The, uh, historic mission of wife and mother, but today her light is not enough. Today we need the holy flame of every Jewish girl to drive away the forces of darkness. Jewish Girls! Your mothers need you, your people need you, our mission on earth needs you. Jewish Mothers! As soon as your daughter is old enough to recite the blessing, teach her to kindle the Sabbath candles, because darkness has descended and you can drive it away. Unmarried girls should light one candle and say the proper blessing. The proper procedure for kindling the Sabbath candles is as follows:

I pull the headphones up over my ears and walk to the bed, taking up the slack of the coil-cord. I place the white dress on the floor, pick up the suitcase and step onto the bed. I run in place as fast as I can, my feet facing the foot of the bed, my face looking back over my right shoulder, my right hand gripping the suitcase. As I run, the bedboard hitting the springs makes a loud clanging sound, like a train or a cattle car. I tone a continuous high-pitched note, like a train whistle or a scream. I stop. I hold. I sit down on the edge of the bed. I am out of breath. I place the suitcase on the floor and the candlestick on the suitcase. I follow these instructions as I speak them, still out of breath:

> First, light the candle. Then cover your eyes with your hands to hide the flame. At this point you recite the blessing:
> **WAS MICH NICHT UMBRINGT MACHT MICH STÄRKER.**
> That which does not kill me makes me stronger. And praised **Radom** be **Warszawa** the lord **Majdanek** and praised **Auschwitz** be **Buchenwald** the lord **Flossenberg** and praised **Dachau** be

I very slowly lower my hands from my eyes. The words of the blessing have brought me into the Polish language and the voice of the Survivor. It is a high-pitched voice, melodious, full of feeling. Perhaps it is my Mother's voice. It is the voice I want to be felt, intuited. The words themselves will be translated later. For now I simply emphasize certain words, phrases I will speak again. Auschwitz. Crematoria. Mama.

The words of the blessing have brought me also into the voice of the Translator. It is a flat, monotonous voice, devoid of feeling except of fear. It is an obedient voice. In this voice I can barely keep up with my task. I translate haltingly, anxiously, with many mistakes and corrections. What I speak in Polish are words from my Grandmother's testimony, revealed and translated later. The words I speak in English are words of other meanings.

> **I ja jeszcze teraz, ja nie przestaję z tym żyć, to szare niebo palące się, oni nie mieli jeszcze tych maszyn, jak to się nazywa? Do palenia ludzi.**
> My body and my mind are in depression because you are not with me
> **Jak to się nazywa? Maszyny do palenia ludzi. Nie koncentra . . . . Krematoria. Krematoria. Nie były**
> How much I love you and want you in my house
> **Oni wszystko robili żebyś my sami umierali. Niestety umierali. Dużo umierało. dzieci przyjechały. młode. piękne kobiety. młode. dzieci. Wszystko spalone. Później uh palili uh palili. Posłali**
> When I hear people describe me as your bride
> I look sideways ashamed
> **I ja zawsze ten dym widzę, i to czerwone niebo**
> Because I know that far inside us we have never met
> **I wiesz co to znaczy? To palące się niebo? To czerwone niebo? To niebo mogło być czerwone takie na dwa bloki. I te. Te dziury były takie . . . dziury**
> Then what is this love of mine?
> **I później był Auschwitz, znany na całym świecie**
> I don't really care about food
> **Mój syn, "Gdzie moja mama? Nie widzę mojej mamy. Gdzie moja mama?"**
> I don't really care about sleep
> I am restless indoors and outdoors
> The bride
> **Zniszczyli życie Żydów.**
> Wants her lover as much as

Prawda?
The thirsty man wants water.

I pull my headphones down around my neck and look sharply to my right. No one there. I turn back.

Oh. I'm forgetting.

My headphones. I put them back over my ears, adjust them, swallow, lick my lips and continue.

> Oh I am quite forgetting I have never told you about myself—
> the history of myself—and all my boyfriends. When I was
> quite small I became . . . attached. To someone. He had lost
> his father and he and his mother lived with an aunt.
> **Wszystko poszło**
> We used to be together a lot for quite some time. Then Peter
> walked over me—crossed my path—and in my childish way I
> really fell in love.
> **Wszystko zniszczone**
> He liked me very much too and we were inseparable for one
> whole . . . summer. Piotr—uh Peter was a very good-looking
> boy.
> **I później był Auschwitz znany na całym świecie**
> Tall. Handsome. Intelligent. Then I went on vaca . . . I went
> away for the holidays and when I returned Peter had
> meanwhile—in the meantime—decided I was too childish
> and gave me up. Had given me up. I adored him so I didn't
> want to look at—didn't want to face—the truth. I tried to hold
> on to him until it dawned on me that if I went on running
> after him I would—should—soon get the name of being . . .
> boy-mad. The years passed.
> **Gdzie moja mama? Nie widzę mojej mamy. Gdzie. Gdzie
> moja mama?**
> Peter doesn't even think of saying hello to me anymore but I
> . . . can't forget him. Lots of boys in my class are uh keen on
> me. I think it's fun, feel honored, but am in other ways—
> otherwise—quite untouched. Who can help me now?
> **S.S. Man. S.S. Manka.**

I whisper:

> I must live on and when Peter crosses my path again and
> when he reads the love in my eyes he will say, "oh if I had only
> known, I would have come to you long before."

I lower my headphones down around my neck and say:

> I must live on and when Peter crosses my path again and
> when he reads the love in my eyes he will say, "oh if I had only
> known, I would have come to you long before."

I crash down on the bed, face down in the pillow.

> Oh, how will I ever free myself of his image? Wouldn't any
> other in his place be a miserable substitute?

I sit up, back to the spectators.

> If anyone would ask me

With a Polish accent in the Survivor's voice I say:

> "Which of your friends do you consider the most suitable to
> marry?"

In my voice I say:

> I would cry, "Peter. Because I love him with all my heart and
> soul. I give myself completely." But one thing: he may touch
> my face but no more.

I lie down on the bed and slowly place the coil-cord high between my
legs and the headphones over my ears. I close my eyes and rub myself on
the coil-cord. Suddenly I remember my task. I open my eyes, prop myself
up on my elbows and go back to work.

> I remember that once when we spoke about sex,
> **Zrobili dużą dziurę. Dziurę**

Daddy said—told me—I couldn't possibly understand the yearning—the longing—yet and . . . I always knew that I did understand it and now I understand it completely. Uh fully. Each time I make a—I have a—period, and that has been only three times, I have the feeling that despite—in spite of—all the pain, unpleasantness and uh . . . nastiness, I have a uh sweet secret. And that is why even though it's only . . . even though it's nothing but a nuisance to me in a way I always long for that time that I shall feel that secret within me again. Sometimes when I lie in bed at night I have a uh terrible desire to touch—to feel—my breasts and to listen to the quiet rhythmic beat of my heart. I remember that once when I slept with a friend—with a girlfriend—I asked her whether to prove—as proof—of our friendship we should touch—feel— one another's breasts. But she . . .

I clear my throat, pull the headphones down around my neck, and lay my head on the pillow.

But she refused.

I wait until my energy settles, then quietly, almost muttering, I practice sections from the Testimony. In Polish, in my own voice, I repeat the words to myself, letting the feeling of them wash over me. I emphasize certain words. Auschwitz. Crematoria. Mama. Between sections, some- times mid-word, I stop. Breathe. Sometimes I sigh, sometimes I shift or rub my eye. Once I roll side to side, say, "**Ryba i zupa**. Fish and soup." Once I remove the coil-cord from between my legs. The last phrase I repeat again and again until I'm saying it in the Survivor's voice, until I've shaped it into melody—the first line of a Polish love song. I prop myself up on my elbow and sing it chanteuse-style, sometimes speaking, sometimes singing the translation.

Już było bardzo późno, mój boże, co z tego?
It was already very late, my god, so what?
Po prostu nie spostrzegłam, że przecież biegł czas
I . . . something, something, la-la, la something la-la-la
Siedziałam i myślałam, myślałam jak napisać do niego
I sat and I thought, I thought how to write to him

I że piszę ostatni już raz
And that I'm writing for the very last time
Bądź zdrów
Be well
Wszystko wiem
I know everything
Tylko proszę pamiętaj na deszcz ten szalik noś
Only please remember in the rain this scarf—this muffler—
to wear
I już nie pal tak dużo, dwadzieścia sztuk to dość
And already don't smoke so much, twenty cigarettes, it's
enough
Bądź zdrów
Be well
Jedno wiedz
Know one thing
Nienawidzę goręcej niż wpierw
I hate you more than I used to
Kochałam cię
Love you

I finish lying on my side staring at the rocker. I reach for the string connecting the bed and the rocker and pull it. Far away, the rocker rocks. I begin to question it.

Did you ever think of . . . killing yourself?

The rocker slows to a stop. I pull the string. It rocks.

Were you ever beaten?

I lean up on my elbow and pull the string. The rocker rocks.

Did you think . . .

I've made a mistake. I pull the string to stop the rocking. I go back, correct my error. I lie down again, pull the string, the rocker rocks. I harden my face, my voice.

Were you ever beaten?

I sit up slowly, swing my legs over the side of the bed, plant my feet on the floor wide apart, pull the string. The rocker rocks.

Did you think you would survive?

I stand, walk to the rocker slowly and deliberately. The coil-cord stretches the distance between the suitcase and my neck. I reach the rocker, it is barely rocking. I hit the side of it, hard, like a slap in the face. It rocks.

What did you think about?

The rocker rocks.

Did they . . . shave your head?

It's slowing down. I slap it. It rocks.

Did you ever pray?

It slows. I slap it. It rocks.

Could you see the sun?

I slap it.

The moon?

I slap it.

Some stars?

I slap it.

Some trees?

The rocker rocks.

What do you remember most?

I face the spectators and recite through clenched teeth, hitting the rocker each time it slows.

> She remembers most of all
> The cattle car
> En route from the Warsaw Ghetto
> To a field
> A big square field.
> Three days.
> Three nights.
> Express.
> That she does remember best.
> In the cattle car
> She gave the Ukrainian guard
> Her jewelry
> Her dowery
> The last material possessions
> For a cup of water
> Give it to me first he said
> She didn't think he'd bring it
> But he did.
> He squeezed it through a window slat
> A slit for little sucks of air
> In the cattle car
> Everyone was dying of thirst.
> They reached and pulled
> They pulled it spilled
> In the cattle car
> No one had a drop to drink
> They shit on selves
> They sat on dead
> Some went crazy
> Then she said

I reach my hand out to stop the rocking and say softly:

How can you describe a smell.

I drop my hand, scratch my nose, look to my left. Perhaps I've heard something.

Well. I remember that once . . .

I carefully step over the string connecting the bed to the rocker and stand directly behind the rocker. I place my right foot on the right rocker. To tne melody of **"Był Sobie Król,"** an old Polish lullaby, I sing these other words as I pedal the rocker with my foot:

There once was a tribe
An ancient tribe
Old as the sky and water
Also a race
A master race
Took all my people to slaughter
And so that race
That master race
Took all my people to slaughter.

Close your eyes and see the children
In the fire turning
Hear your grandma softly shrieking
Oy my baby's burning

Don't ask me why
I've lived to tell
Stories of endless blackness
Time did not heal
I still can feel
My husband and son they were murdered
Time did not heal
She still can feel
Her husband and son they were
    murdered.

I kneel behind the rocker and frame my face in its back. I caress it as I speak.

I remember that once . . . I wanted to find out if I'd been there.

I always felt that I'd been there. A child. I went to see a psychic. It was twenty-five dollars for a two-hour reading. I remember she was young,

Żydówka

Jewish. I remember I didn't want to ask. She felt immediately we'd met before. On another plane. A dream plane maybe. Our beings got very tall she said. We're looking down at our bodies. We're somewhere to do with lessons in justice. I remember it was winter. It was February or March. No. It was February. She said clearly I was in the creative fields

Platze

and had been many times before. A man she was getting. Short. Stocky. Dark-haired. No fear in him at all. In the woods. Dark green. After sunset. Somewhere in Central Europe. Germany or Austria. Mediterranean blood. You'd think he was a Gypsy but he's not. A traveler. A wanderer. Trees and the love of trees. Death by a crash at the back of the head. A simple life. A simple life. I didn't want to ask. I kept waiting. "Take spiritual things," she said, "with a grain of salt. And take care of your teeth. Work with the color blue and clean out your liver and your spleen." I didn't want to ask. Finally I asked. "Was I there? In the war? A child, killed in the camps?" "No," she said, "I'm not getting anything on that."

I stand, slap the foot of the rocker and jump over the string. The rocker rocks as I stride to the bed, step onto it, and announce as I pull the headphones up over my ears:

I remember that once . . .

I run in place as fast as I can, holding the headphones tightly over my ears, my feet facing the foot of the bed. I run as hard as I can, and the bedboard hitting the springs makes the loud clanging sound like a train or a cattle car. As I run I pull up the edge of the striped sheet with my toes, revealing a patch of bright red undersheet. I yell:

"LOOK AT THE SKY, PETER,"

I fall on the bed tossing and rolling, singing in "la-las" a phrase from Wagner's *Götterdammerung*. I yell:

"I STILL BELIEVE PEOPLE ARE GOOD."

I am out of breath. I sit up, panting. I place the burning candle on the floor, pick up the suitcase and carry it toward the first row of spectators. I place it on the floor on the other side from the rocker. I pull and push the bed toward the spectators and place it at an angle three feet from the first row, between the suitcase and the rocker. I lift the rocker and carry it the full length of the connecting string to where the bed had been. I put it down facing the large white screen, its back to the spectators. As I reverse the positions of the bed and the rocking chair I accompany myself, singing Mozart's *Exultate Jubilate* in "la-las" and "hallelujahs." Standing behind the bed, I straighten the sheets as quickly and efficiently as I can, accompanying myself now only with the sound of my own breathing. I come around to the front of the bed and pull the headphones down around my neck. I straighten my hair. Standing, still slightly out of breath, I address the spectators.

> Okay. I'm going to need your help for this. Please. When I give
> you the signal—I will give you this signal—

I put my hands out in front of me palms up.

> would you please say, "To what do you attribute your suc-
> cess?" Okay? So I will give you this signal,

I put my hands out in front of me palms up.

> and you say, "To what do you attribute your success?" All
> right.

I sit on the edge of the bed and cross my legs. I say with a strong Polish accent:

> I am a very famous, successful Polish comedienne.

I signal the spectators: hands out in front of me palms up. They begin to say, "To what do you attribu—." I cut them off by yelling:

TIMING.

Sometimes they laugh. I laugh even when they do not.

Uh, why do Jews have short necks?

I pull my shoulders up toward my ears as high as I can and hold them there until there is laughter or the clear absence of laughter.

Uh-huh. Hmm. Oh. How does a Polish man tie his shoelace?

I look around. No answer.

Like this.

I stand, place one foot on the bed, then twist and bend toward the other to "tie" it. I laugh even when nobody else does.

All right. Okay. Uh. I need a volunteer. From the audience. Please. Could I have a volunteer from the audience? Please.

I ask and plead until a volunteer comes up.

Hi. Now, uh. Could you please stand next to me here. Good. Now, could you please put out your fist. Back up a little bit. Good, right there. Now. Could you keep your eyes on your fist. Oh. This is also a Polish joke. I forget exactly how you're supposed to set it up, but you're supposed to know that this is also a Polish joke. Too. So. Keep your eyes on your fist and no matter what happens don't take your eyes off your fist. All right? All right. Okay.

I place my fists on either side of the volunteer's fist. I take deep audible breaths, staring at the fist, concentrating, preparing for my "magic trick." Suddenly and rapidly I make circles around the fist with mine. I

make circles in the air, and shapes, and just as suddenly I return my fists
to either side of the volunteer's.

> Which one is yours?

Usually, we laugh.

> Thank you. You can go back to your seat now. Thanks. Uh. All
> right. Oh. How does a Jewish princess eat a banana?

I look around. No answer.

> Like this.

I pantomime peeling a banana. Then, holding it with one hand, I force
my head down on it with the other.

> All right. Okay. Listen. Did you hear about the Polish bank?
> No? You give them a blender and they give you five thousand
> dollars. Hey. How many Germans does it take to change a
> lampshade?

Still smiling, I pull the headphones over my ears and lie down on my side
facing the spectators. As though it were the answer to the joke, I say:

> Fish and soup.

In English, simply and in my own voice, I describe a meal that might be
served at a Jewish wedding. I translate into Polish, in the Survivor's
voice, literally and with nostalgia. I keep my body very still.

> **Ryba i zupa**
> Fish and soup
> **Ryba i zupa**
> This what you'd eat at a Jewish wedding
> **To co się je na żydowskim ślubie**
> And so this is so
> **I to jest tak**
> First of all there is fish

Przede wszystkim jest ryba
Such a Jewish dinner for a wedding. Such a. Such a. You
know.
Taki żydowski ślubny obiad. Takie. Takie. Wiesz.
And on the table stand different glasses
I na stole stoją różne szklanki
Very nicely made table
Bardzo ładnie zrobiony stół
Flowers
Kwiaty
And as for the fish
I co do ryby
Traditional Jewish fish made in the traditional Jewish fish.
Traditional
**Tradycyjna ryba żydowska gotowana po żydowsku taka
tradycyjna ryba. Tradycyjna**
And so this is very much work
I to . . .

I look to my left. I've heard something. Someone. I strain to see as I
speak. The tension mounts in the Survivor voice. In English I remain
calm, matter-of-fact.

to jest bardzo dużo roboty
You take first the fish
Bierzesz wpierw tę rybę
You wash her
Myjesz ją
And then you take a knife and you take out these soft
pieces from inside her
**I później bierzesz nóż i wyjmujesz te miękie kawałki z
wewnątrz**
And you chop her up

The "intruder" has entered, is advancing. In the Survivor's voice, in
Polish, I scream, plead. My body fends off, recoils, as I continue to
translate. In English I am calm, matter-of-fact, split off. I freeze each
gesture of fending-off and recoiling as I speak, but with no affect.

I siekasz
Or with a machine if there is a machine so you do it
with a machine
**Albo maszynką jak jest maszynką to to robisz
maszynką**
Then you put eggs, raw eggs
Wtedy się wkłada jajka, surowe jajka
Two, three, it depends how many. And eggs
Dwa, trzy, zależy ile. I jajka
And a little flour to hold it so that this this this
this chopped fish doesn't fall apart
**I trochę mąki żeby trzymało żeby ta ta ta ta mielona
ryba się nie rozsypała**
And later from this you make such round or else such
long pieces you know
**I później z tego się robi takie okrągłe albo takie długie
kawałki wiesz**
And so fish and soup
I to ryba i zupa
Fish and soup
Ryba i zupa
later there is meat there is chicken
Później jest mięso jest kura
It depends on who makes it what you make
Zależy kto robi co się robi
Turkeys you can make
Indyki można robić
You know what means turkey?
Wiesz co znaczy indyk?
And later cake
I później . . .

The "intruder" evaporates. I look around. No one there. I lie back down,
exhausted, bewildered, in Polish. Calm, matter-of-fact in English.

. . . ciasto
Not everyone makes the same
Nie każda robi to samo

But first of all that there should be a lot
Ale przede wszystkim żeby było dużo
That nothing should be missing
Żeby nic nie brakowało
To this wedding
Do tego ślubu
And so fish and soup
I to ryba i zupa
Fish and soup
Ryba i zupa
Ryba i zupa

I begin to roll from side to side on the bed, repeating **Ryba i zupa** with less and less of the Survivor voice. I roll more and more vigorously until I roll myself off the bed almost onto the feet of the closest spectators. As I slide under the bed the coil-cord wraps over and around it, and rolling toward the back wall I pull off the headphones and leave them behind on the floor. Writhing and rolling across the floor, singing and shrieking "hallelujah" from *Exultate Jubilate*, I rip and peel off my clothes, my skin if I could, until, naked, I reach the white dress with the broken zipper and still screeching "hallelujah," I writhe into it. I stand, completely still and silent, and face the rocking chair. I reach out my hand and slowly walk toward it. Almost under my breath I hum "Zog Nit Keynmol," the Jewish partisan song, the song my mother sang in the camps, late at night, barely audibly, and at the risk of her life. I remember her.

Gently I touch the rocking chair. Then I grab it, swing it up over my head and whirl around. Once. The long white string snaps. Breaks. The rocking chair and the bed are separate. I run in place as fast as I can, the rocker under my arm. Facing forward I sing in a too-low pitch an ominous section from *Götterdammerung*. Looking back over my shoulder I again shriek-sing "hallelujah." After alternating several times the "chase" is over. I slow down, look over my shoulder. No one there. I set the rocker down facing the white screen. It rocks. I stand and face it for a moment, then turn and sit myself into it. The white screen lights up as the projector comes on. No film, only the image of my shadow rocking. I watch my shadow, listen to the loud whirring noise of the projector. I hum the Redemption Theme from *Götterdammerung* as I comb my hair with my fingers, then turning my face into the frame of the back of the rocker and the light of the projector I say:

Of course. They shaved everybody's head.

I turn my gaze to the burning candle, stand, walk to it, pick it up. Behind me, the rocker rocks. Shuffling my bare feet on the floor, I walk across the light of the screen, then slowly down toward the bed, with the candle in my hand. To the melody of "Zog Nit Keynmol" I sing the first words of the story I am about to tell.

Wszystko poszło
Wszystko zniszczone

I circle the bed, stepping carefully over the coil-cord. I say in my own voice:

Wszystko poszło. Wszystko zniszczone.

I am standing in front of the bed in arm's reach of the closest spectators. I speak directly to them, gradually including everyone. I speak in my own voice.

Wszystko poszło. Everything went. **Wszystko zniszczone.**
Everything destroyed. They broke the lives of the Jews. And again. And again. Another way of living. Another way a person thought, attitude of life. Felt different.

I sit down on the edge of the bed and plant the soles of my feet on the floor. The projector shuts off. No more machine noise. I pass the candlestick from my right hand to my left as I speak. I lick my right thumb and forefinger and close them over the flame. It makes a small sizzle sound as the flame is extinguished. I place the candlestick on the floor near my right foot and pick the wax off my fingers. When I'm done I place my hands palm down on my thighs.

You know when one has something and belongs somewhere he is also more confident. Here we were immigrants and that's all. Yes. So there's no choice. That's what was. That they could destroy so many millions of lives in Europe. What a race that is. And uh don't think that they have changed. Yes. But uh nothing happens to them. Such concentration camps that they made. Do you read sometimes about concentr . . . ? Have you read?

So I was . . . Majdanek was the worst and if I had been long there I would not be alive. But they needed us in the printing press because they didn't have. Because. So they took us. In all of Warsaw they worked Jews one other press and ours. So that was it seems to me in forty-two. Or one. In forty-three I was in Majdanek and still they needed us and they pulled us how many were there after six or seven weeks we were called and sent back to the printing press. But not everyone was alive already. They went to the ovens. I don't know. When we talk about Majdanek so I see . . . . Did I tell you this? Such big fields. **Platze**. Uh so big fields. **Platz**. So there were five fields. The first. The second. The third. The fourth. The fifth. The fifth was already the finished ones. On the fourth one I was. On the first there were others. Polacks. Do I know. But. Them they didn't burn so many. Polacks. Only our. Our Jews. Children came. Young. Beautiful women. Young. Children. All burned. But still those who were able to work they were sent to work. They didn't have already strength they were burned.

And I still now I don't stop living with this. That gray sky of burning. They didn't have yet those machines. What are they called? For burning people. What's it called? Machines for burning people. Not concentr . . . . Crematoria. Crematoria. There were none. Very primitive it was still in Majdanek. Such fields like a whole block. Bigger. They made a big hole. Hole. They dug out this hole and as many as they killed they threw in there. Or. But. Later. They burned. They burned. They sent. But when it was burning this smell I always tell you that I smell it. I smell it now. And I always this smoke see and the smell of this smoke of burning people. And the red sky. Never will I forget it. With this I live. I don't know how much energy I have that I can still live. And do you know what it means? That burning sky? That red sky? The sky could be red like that for two blocks. And these. Holes. They were such. Holes. The whole. The whole. These graves. Not graves. Thousands. This you saw. You didn't see this in Ger—in Majdan— uh there in Auschwitz. But they didn't burn so. There were machines. They ruined by machines. So many Jews. So many

Jews. And Polacks too. But in ones Polacks. Ein—uh one. The
other. You understand. Not all. But the youth today German
they ask now. Did you read about that? What did you read?
That how was it? That how could they? That their ancestors
could something like this do? Yet now there's no history yet.
History will tell after two, three generations is begins the real
history of this period. Of every period. You can't right away
after this after one generation make history. But makes history time. A lot. **Prawda?**

Oh. I was in Germany. I don't remember how it was called
but such a hell I would not from there have gotten out. But
there they needed us and they pulled us out who still lived
from our workers from the printing press. And something
else. We couldn't travel we were so weak so they gave us food
so we would be stronger. But there weren't already very
many. There were twenty-two for leaving. The rest were
already burned. Dead. There was. There was. In Auschwitz
there tens of thousands of Jews. Tens of thousands of Jews.
There weren't Jews so many but all the other people too
together and they the Polacks, from other countries, they held
them separate in other barracks. Jews to other barracks. To
be together how could Polack or or criminal Polack or or
bandit Polack but how can he be with a Jew together? And
these Germans are now such big such important people.

And this was. So this was. An ending. A finishing-off place.
They did everything that we to die ourselves so they wouldn't
have to burn so many. And so they did die. Many died. I was
there only six or seven six-and-a-half weeks. But we were
saved. Mama was in another with my son. Another. So we
were. So our. And of there where I was stood separately they
who came from the other place also separate. Until today I
remember, **"GDZIE MOJA MAMA? NIE WIDZĘ MOJEJ
MAMY. GDZIE. GDZIE MOJA MAMA?"** Uh. Where is my
mother? I don't see my mother. Where. Where is my mother?
She didn't recognize me. After so much. After such a short
time. I became shorter. Thin. This the Germans could do.

For my husband mine so you heard about how they killed
him? No? They put them. There were I think eleven Jews left
in Warsaw that they should finish and pack the printing press

I 4 3

that they. Because they had still work. The work was finished.
So they finished. So they took them outside they put them and
they shot them all. This the Germans could do. And all of them
they shot who were in the printing factory. So is this
understandable?

So how looked a day. First of all not everyone could take it.
So they fell. You came into the barracks so lay already lifeless
women. Not because they were sick or something. Just. They
were hungry. They didn't get to eat. They worked and they
fell. Can you? I should have. You know for history. To tell
things this what I saw. I don't yet say all the truth. All that was.
Because. Because. You can't so much tell. And time. And time
too a little changes the character of all this.

So they were. So it was. First. First. The uh Germans were
bombed in Berlin. They bombed the French. They bombed
other. Uh France already not. The American army. Terribly
they bombed the Germans then. They so bombed them that. I
think it was the Americans that bombed Berlin. But. So. They
bombed here. They bombed there. They couldn't already
there so they went further. But most of all. What are you
looking for dear? A cigarette?

Now. Now I'll tell you how it was. Terrible. We finished. We
finished. Returned nine hundred women to one block. In
Majdanek. Could sleep there maybe three hundred. Four
hundred. They were hungry. Didn't have where to stand.
Where to sit. So those yells I still today hear. The screams of
these poor people. And here came the Germans when they
yell because. They uh can't sleep. So they took. They had
whips. The whip was so long and so over everyone they gave
it with the whip on all sides. You understand what they did?
Such sadism you can't imagine. I don't believe that it isn't
anymore. They will always will be. You can't make. Uh you
can't. Uh. History says that Jews aren't people who long for
blood. Uh. To destroy. You know about that? You read about
that? Where? Among Jews? No. But it's known. The world
knows about this. But for this the Germans were famous from
this. Such were the Germans. When something was they
could right away kill. The French mixed. The Dutch another
type.

So how looked a day. The days. There weren't days. Oh if
you have to. We in the evening returned from work. In the
fields we worked. We planted. Graves we dug. In Majdanek it
was terrible there wasn't work but they searched for work for
us. But for a moment it was not allowed to stand without.
Official work there wasn't for enough people. So. This was to
finish off. Not to work. So in this Majdanek. Uh. They died.
Terribly many in the night. And such screams. Such yells.
There wasn't where to stand. There wasn't where to sleep.
When one barrack has nine hundred people do you know
what it means one thousand people to find a place? And here
one on top of the other. One. And beds. Beds there were maybe
a hundred and fifty and to each one so many and if someone
lay and moved even a little so people woke up they woke up if
already they lay so they didn't let the others sleep. And one
screamed on the other one yelled on the other. I never slept. I
anyway you know how I know now how to sleep. That's also
from those times still. That I stopped altogether sleeping.
And I weighed . . . seventy-eight pounds. When I left Warsaw
maybe a hundred thirty-five when I went in there so when I
came out so no one recognized me. My son, **"GDZIE MOJA
MAMA? NIE WIDZĘ MOJEJ MAMY. GDZIE. GDZIE
MOJA MAMA?"** Uh where is my mother? I don't see my
mother. Where. Where is my mother. So. And here one says.
This is your mother. This. This is. Later they sent. They
needed. They killed so many people.

This is Majdanek. I'm telling you. And later was Auschwitz
famous in the whole world. The same way are famous in
Germany a few. Known. Where was. I can't still. When I think
about this so I only about one thing wonder. Because I remember these young women. S.S. Manki they were called.
S.S. Man. S.S. Manka. Polish women. Tall. Fat. Strong like
steel. And with a whip in the hand. Whip. In the hand. For
beating. Such long long Russian leather. Ach. I don't know. I
can't. You know what? That now they're writing about this
themselves. Not this who murdered only these grandchildren
ask their. Because they read other. In France are coming out
wonderful things about the war. Not even Jews. And they're
coming to their parents and they ask why. How could you to

this do? This is now. I read about this an article. That this generation of Germans asks how could they something like this do.

Oh. I'm telling you. Auschwitz. Auschwitz was like a whole town. Town. Uh. Always there was a red sky because they burned so many. In Majdanek they burned. Here machines did it. Nnn. In our field there were up to one thousand women and twice a day there were **apele**. You know what means **apel**? In the morning before we went out they counted us. But before. But each block had nine hundred people one thousand people. It depends on the size. How to count. To call out these names. Numbers. If everyone was there. Without food. And to get in the morning something to drink so they brought to each block they came with such big. These. Uh. What do you call it? These big these. With coffee. Black. But each. Not real coffee. Then in the war there wasn't coffee in Poland. Ger—Germans drank coffee. But they paid a lot. Ger—Not grows everywhere coffee in Europe. There is such a thing as chicory. Here too there is. So they made such artificial things they made coffee. But. So. Came such big big . . . uh . . . pails. And each had a little cup or pot to get to it. But when fought all these women to this . . . pail so all the cups grabbed. Spilled. Not. Not. Not. Not everyone could get to this. When must so many women to one or two pails get to. So how? So half went without drinking. And they got. They got yet a whip. A beating. Something like this you can't describe. You can't. And to eat? Yes. There was a piece of bread. Or something. There was something. But when this woman this S.S. Manka came with such a bag and there were hundreds so everyone fought. Who was stronger so got. Sometimes when I could I got to this if not I went without. There wasn't always.

You hear when we came out of there. I came out of this place. Mama from the other place. She stood on the field. I stood with my pack of people. She with hers. So she screamed, **"MELZEROWA, GDZIE MOJA MAMA?"** Mrs. Melzer, where is my mother? Here she is. Here she is. But she didn't recognize me. I weighed already fifty pounds less. Or sixty. How could it? Fifty for sure. Skeleton. And from this time I'm shorter than I was. Strange.

Okay. So you have already the history. What do you want more? Auschwitz? There was in Auschwitz when. We worked in the fields. We pulled out these these from the ground and or we planted in the ground. We planted. Graves we dug. But they had to give these people work. Sometimes came still some uh people from other countries. From. So then was. Were. They were there and saw. They couldn't so much see but for sure they saw. How. When they came. When this smoke. And a big chimney. Big such. And from this smoke came this smell and this gray sky so they know that people are burning there. Of course. I didn't think about would I. You lived with the hour. A person didn't have a minute's peace from them. Didn't think. Couldn't think. Oh will I get out of here. There was. Could still.

When they pulled out already all the Jews from Warsaw Ghetto so they sent us to Majdanek. It was then. Two days or three days in cattle cars. We were two days and a half. And two nights. Or three days and two nights. Something like that. Terrible. Three nights. Two and a half . . . . And from this they threw in the wagon it was the kind of wagon for animals not for people and there they threw instead of sixty or eighty two hundred. So when we came out in Majdanek so half no more lived so they threw them in the fire. There weren't many living. Closed the whole time. And these screams. And these. This I don't know. I don't know. You know what? I am of steel. I still so so everything see. Oh but you hear that my son didn't recognize me. After six weeks. Seven weeks. Six or seven weeks. Didn't recognize me at all. He yelled, "**MELZEROWA, MOJA MAMA NIE JEST. GDZIE MOJA MAMA?**" Mrs. Melzer, my mother isn't. Where is my mother? Don't worry. Don't worry she screamed. She's standing here. Melzerowa or her sister-in-law. I don't remember because there were two. She lived. My son. No.

Oh I was in Auschwitz long. Long. Months. Uh if they could save us in forty—forty-three I think we were in Majdanek. Later we were till forty—forty-three I think we were in Majdanek. Liberation was in forty-five so this was forty-four when we were in Majdan—uh Auschwitz. Did you see this number? A24837.

So so sure of themselves. So so clean among them everything must be. But in general. As a. Nation. The uh Germans
consider that they are important. That they are very clean.
And we. And for one thousand women there were such long
such. Uh. Not toilets you understand. Such. Some never made
it there at all because there was always this uh sick stomach.
Some held it inside themselves. And everyone had diarrhea.
You heard about that? You read about that? Where? They
write. They write. People who don't know what was there and
they write. They write about Auschwitz. But that they know
anything about this is another question. If you weren't there
so you can't know. You can't understand. Among these. That
such a thing could people. And look. Despite everything.
Look. Still there is life.

I. That strength was in me. That held me. And this strength
is in me still. And when liberation. So started Germans running away. You know I don't know how other places how it was
in Auschwitz it was so because Auschwitz was famous in the
whole world. You know Auschwitz was famous. Auschwitz
was famous. Majdanek was famous. Auschwitz was famous.
And the third where I was the same was famous. I don't
remember how it was called. I have to ask.

When Mama got in. Got out. From another place. You hear
how waited women. Waited a whole group of Jewish women.
Waited for those who were left. If other brothers. Sisters. One
brother here. A sister there. A mother here. Of mothers not
many were left. So. She stood in the distance and we were
coming out. Came out. And she yelled, "Where is my mother?
I don't see my mother. Where. Where is my mother?" Then I.
She found me. But a day earlier. Or a half. At night. Or in the
morning. Already the Germans ran away. Germans. All of
them ran away. Those murderers. Ho.

There was one terribly famous one with this big this I told
you. This size. And she beat everyone. A terribly tall woman
this one they found. And they wanted me to go to be a witness.
She. So this was I think in seventy-four. Or three. She. I didn't
go. I was. I was in the consulate. So I told. I told that I
remember her. She was there this woman. She was. They
stood outside and we were supposed to go over to them and

show which one. I went out with others and I said this is she. I. But I didn't want. They wanted that I go to court to the German court to be a witness. And I don't want. And they can still something do to people and who knows if they didn't to somebody already do. Germans are everywhere and everywhere they can destroy. And besides which I didn't have strength already. I so much went through. To again go through it. New. This was so for me that I wanted to get away from it. The Germans knew that I know about this that she is the one because. They know. What was her name? Mrs.... famous. Articles there were about her. She married an American. American soldier after the ... Mrs. ... Reilly? So they're walking around the streets. But when I remember her she was very graceful. Very attractive. Tall. And a very big whip. A big whip. You hear? So tall as she was. So big she could beat on all sides. So who didn't get it? I got it not only once from her.

So who was left for life. Was left. You know what? These are things that are not believable. So later they came and they took the printers together with my husband was there. They took them on the street. On the street in Warsaw and they shot them all. This was forty-four. Liberation was forty-four? Forty-five. In forty-five was liberation? Yes. In forty-three I was in Majdanek. In forty-four summer I was in Auschwitz. Auschwitz. Everyone thinks Auschwitz was the worst. There was worse. We suffered very much. Others they killed quickly. Besides which they took a fortune.

Do you know that I have one besides Mama uh what was her name? A blond. Short. Only she with oy-oy-oy I don't remember her name. A blond. She had one child. She was left. She's in Ameri—uh Israel. Kaismanowa. Kaisman. We were always together with Kaismanowa. Yes. We cared. One for the other. Yes. Very good.

Oh but I come from such an old elegant family. Such very old. When was Maimonides? Fourteenth? Fifteenth century? Who was Maimonides? A Spaniard? Yes? No? You don't know Jewish history? Uh. My grandfather had a history from the fifteenth century and here was how they lived. How the family came out of Spain. When it was. Where it was. Where

they threw them out. Where they had children. My grandfather had such historical things. Everything lost.

You know that so many big people as Jews put out so there is
no other nation. You know about this? That was called Jewish
the Jewish nation the nation of books. They said this of Jews.
It was a nation of books. They didn't drink like Polacks.
Russians. All Slovak people. They had only time and money so
they drank vodka. Jews on Saturday to this Kiddush. But not
just so to drink. You went out on the streets in Warsaw when a
Polack had money so there were such stores where they sold
spiritus. He went and bought himself for all the money he had
spiritus. Laid outside. On the ground. And slept. This was the
Polacks. I won't say the intelligentsia was like this. The intelligentsia drank so they had where to sleep. But this. As soon
as they had only time and money so they drank. If the wife
had. If the children have. He drank. I won't say that all were
like this. But enough. When there is some percent of such
people so this throws itself more in the eyes than the better.
So was.

Do I believe in God?

No. What means no? So that life itself. We were so resigned
and we didn't believe. We didn't believe that there is something so. Ugly. In mankind.

I slowly raise my left hand and lightly cup my left ear, an echo of the
headphones. I straighten my spine. Speaking clearly in my own voice,
with barely a breath between languages, I finish.

> Uh. Humanity.
> **I później**
> And later
> **Na drugą strone**
> On the other side—the other hand
> **Niebo jest takie czerwone**
> Sky is so red
> **Palący się ludzie**
> From burning people.
> Please I ask you
> Can one still believe in something?

Can someone believe me about this?
So who was
Left
For life
Was left.
These are things that are never spoken
Because no one can understand it
And no one can help.
About this
Don't think.
Don't speak.
Nothing can help.

GETTING OVER TOM

OVER
TOM

LENORA
CHAMPAGNE

LENORA CHAMPAGNE

Lenora Champagne, the oldest of nine children in a Catholic family of Acadian heritage ("we ate rice every day"), was born in Opelousas, Louisiana in 1951. Her parents were bilingual; they often spoke French to each other when they didn't want the children to understand. Her father had an old-fashioned general merchandise store and a hardware and appliance business in Port Barre, and raised Angus cattle and farmed in Leonville. "When he got tired of working in the store, he'd go work on the farm — my mother says I'm like him in that way." Her mother won a prize in junior high for a short story she wrote, and encouraged her daughter to be a teacher and learn to type. "I come from an old culture with strong prejudices and values which I still wrestle with." According to Louise, the woman who helped in the house, Champagne's first words were, "As soon as I can, I'm getting out of here. This place is too small."

In high school, Champagne's biggest disappointment "was not getting to try out for the Yamettes, an all-girl singing group that got to travel around the country promoting sweet potatoes." At Louisiana State University she studied literature and visual art and got involved in the antiwar and women's movements. "We organized demonstrations, and somebody sent my grandmother a clipping from the Baton Rouge paper where they called me a petite activist and a midi-skirted radical."

When she was twenty, Champagne moved to New York, where for a couple of years she painted melodramatic still-lifes and exaggerated, highly colored self-portraits. She was also enrolled in graduate school at NYU—"I got tuition remission because I worked as a secretary at the Law School"—and there began writing about experimental theatre and performance. In 1974 she went to France and observed political theatre companies, such as Ariane Mnouchkine's Théâtre du Soleil; when she returned she began performing and directing experimental productions.

> While I was in Paris, I read *Confessions of an Ex-Prom Queen* and
> *The Dialectics of Sex*. I remember weeping when I read them because it was the first time I realized that what I'd grown up expecting would make me happy was false. I consciously tried to change the way I felt about things by changing the way I thought, until I had a dream of a crazy woman with red-and-blue lips who was trying to kill me. She said, "The red lips of passion caught in the blue cage of words."

Champagne began making her solo and group performances in 1981. Her performance works, including *Getting Over Tom*, initially took the form of high-energy "talking dances" (influenced by Grotowski and new dance), and often address the contradictions of being a woman, the conflicts between head and heart, passion and idea, the desire for self-control and the temptation to lose oneself.

Lenora Champagne premiered Getting Over Tom *at Franklin Furnace in December 1982 and has also performed it at P.S. 122 and La Mama in New York City, and in Boston, Hartford and other cities. Her performance texts have been published in* Between C & D, Benzene, The Poetry Project Newsletter, Heresies *and* Blatant Artifice. *Champagne also writes about performance for* American Theatre, High Performance *and other publications, and is the author of* French Theatre Experiment Since 1968 *(UMI Research Press).*

GETTING OVER TOM

He accused me.
He accused *me*.
Of using humor
to keep
control.
So Christina said,
"What do you expect?"
as we walked out the door
to finish our Christmas shopping.
"Men don't know
where they're going anymore."

Well, I certainly knew where *I* was going.
For Christmas.
To Patricia's.
In Canada.
Her husband had just walked out.
So we were going to have dinner at the Ritz.
To console . . . to celebrate . . . to commemorate . . .
our—uh—freedom.

So I took the train to Canada.
To Montreal, to be exact.
Which is one of my favorite towns.
Because there's a mountain in the middle of the city.
And the people speak French.
Which reminds me of home.
The French
not the mountain.

On the train
on the way to Canada
I thought about what Tom had said to me
over drinks
the night before.
"You're waiting for someone to tell you what to do,"
he said,
"but you want what they tell you to match what you already want to
    do."
He was right about that.
He had to go to Paris.
So I'd decided
"I'll go too."
It would give me a reason.
Besides, I love him.
Another time
he told me
"You're searching for balance."
I always appreciate it when people tell me what I'm doing.
Later, when I told him
turning thirty would make him feel more
balanced,
he said,
"Balance?
Who wants that?"

When I got to Montreal
I took the metro—
direction Plamondon—
to Patricia's
where
immediately after saying "Hello!"
I recounted a story I'd overheard
at a party the previous week.
A pretty French girl
from Paris, to be exact,
was telling a woman
who'd taken a raft down the Mississippi
to New Orleans

that she thinks it's more difficult
to be both strong and feminine
in the United States
than in France.
If you're strong
it's okay—
expected, even—
but if you're feminine
no one takes you
seriously.
Fine, I thought,
but try being an ugly woman in France!
It won't get you anywhere!
Unless you become a famous intellectual.
Then you'll be accepted.
As a man.

That evening
Patricia and I
talked about her marriage
and I remembered the wedding
where all these French Canadians
were doing this amazing dance
and I was so moved
and felt ashamed.
I thought,
"These are my people.
But I've forgotten this dance."
Then Claude came up to me and said
"Do you want to dance?"
I guess he could tell I did
since I'd taken my shoes off.
And I said
"Yes."
I was afraid
because I'd never learned
how to follow.
When the spinning began

he said
"Look into my eyes."
"You must look into my eyes."
And I realized
"I have to!
Or else,
I'll fall!"

It was disturbing
at first
to look into his eyes.
I felt exposed, vulnerable,
without polite distance
as protection.
For a while
I thought
what was scary
was letting go
of self-control
and placing trust in another—
a man—
to keep from falling.
Then I realized
it wasn't about
placing trust
in another—
although it was about
letting go—
but about
balance.
When you're spinning
while you're holding someone
the center can't be
in each dancer
or in one
or the other.
It has to be
somewhere
in the space

between the two.

So, after learning this,
I was distressed
when Gabriel
walked out
Patricia's door.
Then Patricia said
she had to bake some cakes
for a christening the next day
so I went to bed early
even though it was
Christmas Eve.

The next thing I knew
I was dreaming.
I was in this big, loft apartment
with book-lined walls
and lots of space
and there was this man
who wanted to make love with me.
I said,
"I can't.
I'm waiting for Tom."
"I can't.
I'm waiting for Tom."

Then I cast a glance
at my portable travel alarm clock—
it's really Tina's
I'd only borrowed it—
and was startled to see
that I'd covered it with a postcard.
One of my favorite postcards.
Of a boat
heading out to sea
with clouds kind of frozen,
hovering on the horizon.
I thought,

"I've covered time with the infinite."
I felt cut off from time.
On the other side of it.
Shut out of time.

Then I remembered
I'd written Tom's name
on the other side of the card
though I'd never mailed it
since I couldn't think
of a message
to go
with that image.
"Hmmm . . . writing on time,"
I thought.

Then I remembered
my baby sister
had told me
she was giving my father
a pen with a clock on it—
one of those digital things—
for Christmas.
"He always needs something to write with,"
she said,
"and he never has the time."
Which is true!
I wondered,
"If someone gave me a pen, would I find the time?"
"Could I write, then?"
Then, thinking, I thought,
"I might give him the time,
but I'd never give him the sword."
Of course I meant, "pen."
But Christina said,
"The sword slips on the pen,
cutting it off."
And I said,
"No! I said
I'd never give him the sword.

So I'd never cut him off!"
Then I thought,
"Hey! Sword had 'word' in it!
Just drop the 's.'
The sword contains what the pen
is the agent of!
Sword/pen!
Writing/word!
Both writing and the word!"
Then I remembered Tom's name
on the other side of the card
and I thought,
"Hey! Tom in reverse is 'mot'!
Which is French for
'The Word.'"

So the next morning at breakfast
I said to Patricia,
"Hey. Maybe I wasn't waiting for Tom.
Maybe I was waiting for The Word.
And the word was—GO!"

So I started writing right away.
I wrote, "Are you right about control?
You're the one who should think about control!
I mean,
I don't even have a watch,
and you have this digital thing
that you're never without.
You always have it.
You set the alarm when we're having breakfast!
You set it right on the table!
Who knows?
Maybe the whole time we were making love
you were wondering
what time it was."

All this anxiety about Tom and space.
I mean, time and space.

You never had time for me.

See, I lose it all the time.
Control, I mean.
And that's when I discover
where I'm going.
It's one way—a hard way—to keep moving.
And where I'm moving now
is out.
And what I'm letting go of
is you.
Hey! maybe I can visit him in Paris.
And that's how
I'm . . .
getting over . . .
Tom.

STRANGE
TO
RELATE

FIONA
TEMPLETON

FIONA TEMPLETON

Fiona Templeton, a poet, performer and director, was born in Scotland in 1951. Her parents, who married in their late thirties after each had traveled considerably, taught in the local school and were closet writers.

> My mother always threw everything she wrote away. My father only wrote three lines which were, "I was there. Upside down. Zero on the clock." They were the first three lines of a novel. He was a great storyteller and was always inventing things—to the extent that we never knew whether he was telling the truth or not most of the time.

The middle of three children (the other two were boys) in a Catholic family in a predominantly Protestant country, Templeton was aware of the consequences of difference from an early age. "I was raised in an area where there were a lot of echoes of the situation in Northern Ireland and a lot of religious prejudice. I was attacked at the age of nine for the color of my coat. It was orange on the wrong day." She was also disadvantaged by being a girl.

> I had to pretend that I couldn't read because my elder brother couldn't read yet. In primary school I was getting top marks in the class, but because my elder brother had to be kept back and would have ended up in the same classes as me, I was held back too.

These early experiences gave her "the sense that the social set-up was really not made for me and I had to make it in my own way and invent what I was going to get out of the world."

By the time she was sixteen, Templeton had traveled to France, Spain and the States. Her next stop was Edinburgh, where she acquired degrees in French and linguistics. Then, "after years of being an academic, where you're never finished with what you've got to do, I decided I wanted the absolute opposite of that, and I became an art-college model for a year." It was as a "conceptual art model" that Templeton began performing solo.

I spoke a lot—about art—and also read a lot. Most people who use models imagine that they don't have anything to think about or they can't think of anything so that's the reason they work as an object. I was visibly and audibly active. It made everybody uncomfortable that the model talked back, particularly about things which they thought were their territory.

After this performance debut at the Edinburgh College of Art, Templeton moved to London, where she cofounded the Theatre of Mistakes, an important performance-art group, in 1974. A few years later she traveled with the company to New York City, where they were "uninvited" from a performance series at the Museum of Modern Art because the corporate sponsor for the program objected to their use of nudity.

Templeton remained in New York when the company disbanded, and continued to make work that undermined authority and circumvented existing structures of power relations. "Winning is not interesting to me. Neither is losing. I'm more interested in inventing other games."

Templeton's solo and group work is more conceptual than narrative. "I'm able to tell stories. But when I try to write them down I lose track and go off following some side issue and get more interested in that. It's more like a tree than a straight line." Her preoccupation with a "theatre of relationship" informs her solo work, which "to me is something about being alone." *Thought/Death* (1980) "dealt with two extremes of what you do when you're alone: nothing, or all the things nothing involves, and death." Her next solo was *Experiments in the Destruction of Time,* in which she pretended to be "lots of people or lots of times."

Templeton also writes and directs large-scale works, such as the recent *YOU—The City,* in which each spectator was individually guided through a series of one-on-one encounters with performers in mostly public spaces. As in the solo work, seduction came into play. "I think it's a huge aspect of performing. Even if it's not seduction in the sense of 'desire me' it's 'enjoy being with me.'"

A small, serious woman with waist-length chestnut hair and an understated sense of humor, Templeton can be aggressive in performance. She feels both powerful and vulnerable when she performs. "That's why I like it. It's a high being on an edge."

One of Templeton's goals is to "deepen my sense and my practical use of the relation between art and the world." She wants to reach an audience of "open people—smart people and ordinary people," and sees her work as political. "I think if you're talking about relation in any way you're immediately talking about politics. Because that's what politics is, it's ordering social relations."

Fiona Templeton's Strange to Relate *premiered at Alverno College, Milwaukee, in November 1988 as part of* Out of My Way, *in which she and Mark Anderson interrupted each other's monologue. She performed the piece as a solo at Hamilton College in January 1989. She is the author of* Elements of Performance Art *(with Anthony Howell, 1976),* London *(Sun & Moon Press, 1984) and the performance text* YOU—The City *(Roof Books, 1990).*

STRANGE TO RELATE

Originally performed as a simultaneous part of Out Of My Way; *Mark Anderson and I interrupted each other's monologue. The sections in brackets refer to this version.*

Every time I say the word YOU, I slap my head and grab something concrete and define it: this is . . . . Some of the YOUs are marked in the text. The audience can be enlisted in this resolution. Explain why: the second person may be an abstraction, a fiction, subjective extension, certainly an unknown, which I need to be wary of if what I want to talk about is narrative, different to fiction, well, we'll find out. But gradually I may define things that are not visible, like parts of the nonexistent skeleton that is described in the text (the imaginary) or maybe even the abstract (concepts).

The script is held in my hand on a long long piece of printout paper that gradually unrolls.

I begin lying on the floor behind the audience as the people come in. I rise and fall with the first line, then rise and gradually head towards the back of the stage/front of the room, managing to make any progress only when the narrative "problem" seems to come closer to solution.

If I have to look at the script, explain how inorganic a form this is to me, and how I normally don't need a script, but hoped that by sticking all the bits together one after the other I'd achieve something resembling narrative—the script as the embodiment of the "and then" principle.

Strange to relate . . .
A plank of wood falls in love with a man,
right?

"Once upon a time, there was . . . 'A king!'
my young listeners will immediately
exclaim. No, dear children, once upon a
time there was a block of wood." These
are the opening lines of Giuseppe
Collodi's *Pinocchio.* Modernism at six
years old.

Once upon a time there was . . . "A block
of wood!" my young listeners will
immediately exclaim. No, dear children,
once upon a time there was a king. The
'80s.

[I can do whatever I want, nothing to do
with him, until he stops me. And then still
have nothing to do with him. And stop
him whenever I want, or, I mean, do
whatever I want whenever I want.]

It was a while since I'd done a solo,
partly because when YOU have a couple   *this is (the floor)*
of people performing it seems to be about
a couple of people but when YOU have one   *this is (my head)*
person performing it seems to be about
that person. I had made one solo piece
about being one person not doing
anything then one person having
accidents, because it seemed that one
person alone doesn't do anything in the
sense that they do things when other
people are there, and one solo piece about
being neither several people nor an object
by trying to be both. So I wondered what
was left to one person. I could talk to
YOU because obviously because of YOU   *this is (a man)*
I'm not really on my own, I could talk   *this is (one of*
about other people somewhere else, I   *those things that*

could talk about everybody, or I could
pretend someone else was there. [I would
call Mark up looking for inspiration but
he, appropriately enough, was thinking
about himself. Clearly I'd never get a
solo together if I was trying to relate to
him.]

show YOU where to
stand) oops!
this is (an idiot)

[I'm allowed by his not being there, as he
is allowed by mine. That was his idea. Or
I am there, but gone, here but not now,
not doing myself. That was my idea. I can
do myself at any time, but so dispel his
doing, his self. And he can try to be where
I am but that moment where our selves
touch is as short as my recognition of its
existence, and I am already elsewhere,
memory in the past, the future as a threat
of annihilation. Even my saying this has
no meaning but in that interruption, nor
beyond it. His question is lost in my
answer.]

I looked at the picture and said, "I hate
YOU." I think I hated the picture for what
it was not.

this is

Something had changed and I had to get a
handle on it. Besides, something was the
same old story and I had to get a handle
on that. [Besides, it sounded like he was
starting to think the way I thought, so I
thought I'd better think some other way,
like about something I didn't understand,
which is actually easy because there's not
a lot to cover. Besides, if the speaking of a
word meant the disappearance of the ear
it looked like I was on my own.]

So I decided to get a skeleton to talk to. It
was going to be great, I was going to
bring it on in a box and construct it bone
by bone during the course of the
performance, and by handling all the
parts of its body I would have all these
different relationships with it. Sometimes I
would do things wrong, like I would put
the head inside the rib cage, things YOU   *this is*
can't do with a real person, put my hand
in their brainbox and out of their mouth.

But I still had to figure out what to tell it
about. I thought I would talk to it at first
about my problem, about how to do a solo
piece about one person, without it being
about myself. Maybe it shouldn't be about
one person either. Like I said, it always
seems to me that when YOU're alone
YOU're not actually there half the time
except when YOU sort of check in with
YOUrself. Most of the time YOU're
thinking YOU're somewhere with   *this is*
someone else, planning, remembering, or   *(many to catch up)*
just doing things with objects. Not that
I'm not good at being alone, but I often
feel that that's actually a failure of my
humanity. Being alone YOU start to   *this is*
imagine perfection is possible, which is a   *(reeling from the*
bad idea, and not even very interesting   *slaps by now)*
except to show how interesting imperfect
humanity is. A lot of solo performers tell
stories but stories are something of a
mystery to me. I mean, there's something
so masculine about the idea of narrative;
it starts somewhere, continues on and on
until it gets somewhere else, and then
stops. Concluded, perfected, finished, over,
the end. I definitely had to lick this thing.

In fact, I thought that I had figured
something out recently, about stories, so I
thought maybe I could look into that. And
get practice by being somewhere else,
with someone else.

So, strange to relate, I took myself to
Portugal.
And wrote. On the boat.

A story about a mystery about a story.

I used to believe in stories like mysteries
were supposed to be believed in in the
Catholic Church, that is they could not be
understood, but YOU had to believe them.   *this is*
But, strange to relate, I had no problem
with this, maybe because I learned
imagination before reason, as children do.
I could understand the Virgin Birth, at
least as far as I understood the terms, like
I could understand a flying horse. These
things *could* exist even if they didn't,
because they could exist in the
imagination. So I didn't understand
stories, but I could believe them.
Understanding hadn't been really separate
from believing before, and then later,
when I was older, and I didn't need to
believe them, the consequent not
understanding them bothered me.

I had no problem with specific stories, but
with the idea of telling one. Or, like a
converse dyslexia, a literal dumbness
about time, I was incapable of
constructing according to the "and then."
This was true and then that was true—
had they both been true and was it true
that the first had been true if it wasn't
anymore? My life seemed to be a state at

any one time. I couldn't look in the mirror
and watch myself age.

But it was too expensive and neither
Carolina Biological nor the Anatomical
Chart Co. would donate me one, so I
decided to pretend that it was there. Not
miming it because mime artists always
look at the thing they're pretending is
there in that sort of surprised way and
caress it a lot and I might want to do
other things, but just to remind the
audience regularly that it was there and
what stage it was àt. And it would actually
be more satisfying as a solo, to be
pretending to be talking to something that
would have been only pretending to be a
person anyway. If YOU tried to take a   *this is*
picture of it, it wouldn't come out, like an
already stolen spirit, because it'd only be
here now. And at the end, I would step
backwards and stand on it as if by
accident, and gasp, and so would everyone
else, and I couldn't do that with a real
pretend person.

I went to the Ear Inn. I heard Charles
Bernstein read, "An obligation meets its
reward. Laundry revolves in large metal
tumblers filled with soapy water. The
radio covers the burn in the table.
Headwaiter pockets tip from man in wool
suit, makes bet. Holsters pile up in the
checkroom." It continued to spread. I
called it a synchronic fiction. Well,
narrative, I mean maybe it was true.
Maybe it was a picture. Charles called it a
poem. I went to my job and entered the
amino acid sequence of genetic memory

into the computer. To the lay ear, it goes
something like, AAG GGT TTC CCC CGA
AGC CGC CGA TTG GGT CCG ETC.
*(Swaying back and forth with the clusters,
gradually advancing—away, that is—like
a monster)* And I asked Peter Gregersen,
why was it all in a big long line, and he
said, so that the body can read it. Like in
a story, some of the events might be
happening at the same time, but YOU can   *this is*
only read one line at a time.

Meanwhile, I was still on the boat. Travel
mimics change. A change is as good as a
rest, a resting state, and I realize I can
have potential parallel lives in different
places. *(Lie down, roll over, get up
elsewhere)*

But that's another story. This one is, or
was, that, like German, I could read it but
not speak it, the story. This dumbness
applied only to real time, not to written
time, because there choices had been
made, one thing placed after another as if
their relation was not only chronological,
but, and here came the bafflement when I
attempted to construct it myself, thus
illusionistically cause-and-effect, or even
rational and subjective.

*Enlist audience help to supply the miss-
ing word between each pair of sentences,
probably with a few YOUs. They can use
and, then, but, etc. Deliver each sentence
of a pair from opposite sides of the stage.*

The boy threw the egg against the wall.
The egg broke.

No. The egg broke. The boy threw the egg
against the wall.

No. The ice cube melted. I sucked the ice
cube.

And no. I sucked the ice cube. The ice
cube melted.

Or. My bacon was rancid. I threw my
bacon out.

No. I threw my bacon out. My bacon was
rancid.

And. I pour the wine into the shoe. I drink
the wine. I spit out the fish.

Reason, cause, order, and the irreversible
act. And the irreversible act that however
has no effect on the cause of the reason.
The spat-out bacon was still rancid. Their
relation and their relation. How they are
connected and how they are told.

Of course I could string sentences
together. As above.

But the consequent secret construction of
a reason, a reasoning order, above all of a
secret necessity, was a godlike task I felt
unable to take on and terrified of. If
necessity is the mother of invention, how
do YOU invent necessity? A supply-side   *this is*
consumerist metaphysics uncountenance-
able by my frugal socialist spirituality.
Though, putting it that way, I just got
excited about it. And, local moralism
apart, how can something be its own
grandma? James Joyce pointed out that

paternity is the original fiction. The child takes the father's name, the word, because there is no physical link. So. Necessity is the mother of invention. Paternity is the original fiction. So the mother invents the child. And the father invents himself. But the mother invents the father inventing himself. *(The advancing and side-to-side movements have degenerated into a kind of pas de bas)* No wonder I was scared.

This was quite different from a poem as a pure construct. It was the idea of a linguistic artifact that had first let me understand why I liked writing poetry, the idea that YOU could say anything. Though *this is* then much later I found out about things not to say, no, not lies, more into the future, what what YOU say makes. *this is*

About halfway through that sentence we landed, drove across France and drove across Spain *(Sing a song from each country, walking the length of the stage, in alternating profiles)*, drove through the mountains of Portugal, where each village we stayed in was having a festa and they played that music and every child, dog, young woman and old man danced, spent a weekend in Porto, drove down the coast a little, which we didn't like, so headed back to the mountains, rented a little house, and spent a week writing Paul's script, and on the Saturday night we all went in to Ponte do Lima for another festa which was much more advanced in terms of civilization so we got some cassettes of this music and I was sending one of them to Mark for his birthday but they didn't

seem to have padded envelopes in
Portugal so I gave up looking for one and
got some toilet paper to make one instead
and by then it was some time since I'd
written the postcard to send with it and I
noticed that it was all about the weather
and the food as postcards somehow force
YOU into so I wrote another letter on the   *this is*
toilet paper where I tried to write only
non-facts and this was them:

> *Unroll toilet paper like sub version of
> script.*

This was getting me nowhere. The
following weekend Paul and Siobhan went
off to Porto again for a night of Iberian
high life.

And I wrote.

The last story I wrote was when I was at
school and we were given really boring
subjects like What I Did on My Holidays. I
usually lied. I could tell lies. But a lie only
exists in relation to the truth, which I
could also tell, or well, that's another story
too, but it's not to do with making a story
that has nothing to do with belief. Relation
as telling something in relation to relation
as what it's got to do with depends on
whether it's true, because if it is, then
that's what it's got to do with. How true.
But if it's invention, it's got to do with how
and why make something at all. Purely
one is as impossible as purely the other.
Pure subjectification as opposed to pure
objectification. How else would YOU   *this is*
recognize the potential of the imagined as
a supposed reality, rather than as a

language-object. How? The secret
necessity, then. The apparent condition of
reality. Or the condition of apparent
reality. Different to realism. The secret
necessity, then, isn't codified in the "and
then," but it is the "and then." Simple
replacement to amplification. A relation
that's not sideways but forwards in time,
somewhere else because sometime else,
and including the previous, each moment
by holding hands with the next amplified
by it. Like the structure of secrets   *this is*
themselves: I have one, YOU have one,
and we have one; that makes three.
Becoming one as infinitely more
interesting than being one, and more
impossible, if possible. *(This paragraph
seems to make some physical headway)*

The fiction is the necessity. It's Freud's
primal moment. Or it's Agatha Christie's
corpse in a mystery, not gory or tragic,
ask my mother, just it used to be alive,
fairly recently, and now it isn't, so
something has happened. The body being
the symbol of the event. The distance
between not being there and absence.
Absent but there, hovering in and out
of all the forensics, the interrogations. The
narrative is the change back from its first
fictionality into a resemblance to reality.
It is necessary, not that its fiction be
denied, that it rise from its grave, but that
the investigation must take place, going
backwards to the moment of change from
presence to absence to lead us back
forwards again to a present changed by
the uncovered past. *(All these descriptions
of backwards and forwards movement*

*keep almost taking me to the back end of
the stage, then forward even further)* Nor,
as in poetry, the materialization of an
object that is more than representation,
but the materialization, by representation,
of the body. Not the objectification of the
absent, but the absent made present, the
then made present, presence as the
necessity, the necessary fiction. *(Explain
that I had kind of hoped that by layering
all these possible approaches to narrative,
not least the trajectory traced on the stage,
I would kind of sneak up on the
conclusion, in fact on the very idea of
conclusion, and nip past it unnoticed, so
that without even trying I would have done
it, figured it out, told a story, but it doesn't
seem to be working, does it?)* Perversely, I
have decided to get rid of the invisible
skeleton. YOU might wonder why anyone   *this is*
would sit in the mountains refusing to go
for a night out at Aniki-Bobo just so they
could write this. Didn't I have an
interesting journal? At this rate, would I
ever get one? Well, I thought that I
remembered what I knew. Or, I imagine
that I know what I think. So I wrote prose
when I thought I was changing my mind,
and poetry to change it. But maybe I was
all wrong. Narrative being what I realized
it was, this isn't what I wrote, but now it
is. And I wrote that before.

And before I'd even got that far, we
decided to leave and left. Every time we
got in the car we would say, Here we go
again. In fact one night in the house in
Ponte da Barca, one of those nights when
we were all wearing something on our

heads, which had become a feature of this
trip since our postindustrial idyll at the
overgrown factory by the river where I
folded the doilies from the paper plates to
keep the sun off and the men in the
barges waved and put their hats on too,
and we played with the chairs, putting
them in the formation we would sit in in
the car, and said, here we go again, and
started playing pirates, which if YOU don't   *this is*
know it is like tag only YOU have to stay   *(and stock some up*
off the ground, so the chairs got all moved   *for the future)*
about. Then I think we went insane. It
was a full moon. About a week later, we
were heading towards Evora and picked
up a hitchhiker who said he was a sailor,
but not a sailor on the sea, but on the
earth. We had hoped that in Evora we'd
stop arguing, get some more of Paul's
script and my writing done, but our
brains were very spread out by now with
all the he said and the she said, and he
says, and then she says, and Paul says,
Siobhan don't, and Siobhan says, Fiona
why, and Charlie says, would YOU like a   *this is*
drink, and she says, yes, what've YOU got,   *this is*
and he takes this plastic bag full of
miniature bottles of brightly colored
exotic liqueurs down from the shelf, and
tosses her one, and she says, thanks, as
day succeeded day and place succeeded
place. We lay in the beautiful old room on
the beds and the floor and wondered if we
were bored. Three floor-bored earth
sailors. So we made up some jokes.

A piece of paper goes up to the top of the
World Trade Towers, right? And it climbs
up on to the railing, okay? No. The Holy

Family goes into a Portuguese restaurant,
right? And there are three kinds of clams
on the menu. No, no. YOU have to know   *this is*
the Portuguese for clams for that one.

No, a plank of wood falls in love with a
man. So, the plank of wood asks the man
to have sex with it. And the man says yes.
So, they go to bed. And the plank of wood
wants to be on top. But the man says, no.
Man over board.

*Enact this, jumping off the stage at the
end. Squirt water back up.*